"I'm happy to endorse the Join 1 Million Me[...] series. Pornography is an epidemic that has para[...] forward in a walk with God, and from serving as church leaders. This aggressive project should raise the bar for countless men who have been caught in the web of pornography. By God's grace, it will help them find a Christ-centered repentance and transformation that will liberate and empower them, their families, and churches."

—RANDY ALCORN, author of *The Purity Principle* and *Heaven*

"Pornography is not a harmless addiction. It is often a root that leads to broken marriages, child abuse, and physical harm—leaving a trail of victims in its wake. Dr. Jay Dennis's Join 1 Million Men in the War Against Pornography is a wonderful ministry that seeks to set men (and women) free from the destruction of pornography. His heart for God and his desire to restore purity to men and women in the church drives Dr. Dennis's vision. And his call for One Million Women Praying to see the church porn free is one that we gainfully support."

—SHARI RENDALL, director of legislation and public policy,
Concerned Women for America

"My friend Jay Dennis has a great and tender heart for ministry at its elemental and most human levels. May God bless his important and abiding work. May the healing and help Jay is offering be providentially restorative."

—TIM GOEGLEIN, vice-president of external relations, Focus on the Family

"Pornography is a cancer, destroying lives and ruining families. Jay Dennis is a wise and careful surgeon, using the fine scalpel of God's Word to help men gain victory over this moral disease. It's my hope that fully 1 million men and even more will find hope and healing through this outstanding resource."

—ROBERT F. SCHWARZWALDER JR., senior vice-president,
Family Research Council

Join 1 Million Men in the War Against Pornography Includes

Join1MillionMen.org

Our Hardcore Battle Plan A–Z

Our Hardcore Battle Plan App

Our Hardcore Battle Plan DVD

Our Hardcore Battle Plan Commitment

Our Hardcore Battle Plan for Wives: Winning in the War Against Pornography

OUR HARDCORE BATTLE PLAN

Joining in the War Against Pornography

JAY DENNIS

NEW HOPE
PUBLISHERS
Gospel-Centered. Missions-Driven.

BIRMINGHAM, ALABAMA

New Hope® Publishers
P. O. Box 12065
Birmingham, AL 35202-2065
NewHopeDigital.com
New Hope Publishers is a division of WMU®.

Library of Congress Control Number: 2013935926

All Scripture quotations, unless otherwise indicated, are taken from the New American Standard Bible®, Copyright © 1960, 1962, 1963, 1968, 1971, 1972, 1973, 1975, 1977, 1995 by The Lockman Foundation. Used by permission.
   Scripture quotations marked (AMP) are taken from the Amplified® Bible, Copyright © 1954, 1958, 1962, 1964, 1965, 1987 by The Lockman Foundation. Used by permission.
   Scripture quotations marked (*The Message*) are taken from *The Message* by Eugene H. Peterson. Copyright © 1993, 1994, 1995, 1996, 2000, 2001, 2002. Used by permission of NavPress Publishing Group."
   Scripture quotations marked (NIV) are taken from the HOLY BIBLE, NEW INTERNATIONAL VERSION®. NIV®. Copyright©1973, 1978, 1984 by International Bible Society. Used by permission of Zondervan. All rights reserved.
   Scripture quotations marked (NLT) are taken from the *Holy Bible*, New Living Translation, copyright © 1996. Used by permission of Tyndale House Publishers, Inc., Wheaton, Illinois. All rights reserved.

Web site URLs provided accessed April 2013.
Cover design: Casscom
Interior design: Glynese Northam
Special thanks to: Mark Bethea, Dave Huggins, Adam Smith

ISBN-10: 1-59669-370-3
ISBN-13: 978-1-59669-370-8

N134111 • 0613 • 5M1

*D*edication

I dedicate this book to every man who takes the challenge

and says, "I will live a pornography-free life."

*T*able of Contents

Acknowledgments

Beyond my experiences with the needs at First Baptist Church at the Mall, I studied the facts about sexual addiction, in the process obtaining certification in sexual addictions through the Institute for Sexual Wholeness, Atlanta, Georgia.

Institute leadership—Dr. Michael Sytsma, Dr. Dough Rosenau, and Debra Taylor—were phenomenal examples of godliness and excellence in addressing a sensitive issue.

Dr. Mark Laaser, a pioneer in Christian sexual addiction issues, encouraged and helped me to learn even more. I am so grateful for him and his Faithful and True Ministries. The materials he writes along with his lovely wife, Debra, are excellent and useful.

Along the way, Craig Gross of XXXChurch has been very helpful in sharing wisdom and counsel. God is greatly using him.

Luke Gilkerson and the staff team at Covenant Eyes have been an incredible encouragement to me in this process and I cannot thank them enough for their counsel.

I want to thank Tanis Leo, a prayer warrior from Canada, who spoke words of encouragement and affirmation that this ministry could touch the world.

Thank you, Pastor Tim Osiowy and Gateway Christian Ministries in Prince George Island, British Columbia, for gathering around me and praying God's anointing and protection.

Thank you to so many others who are committed to this movement; as I travel, speak with, and work alongside you in this movement, I am grateful to see how God is using you for His glory.

A special thank-you to what I believe is the greatest church on earth, First Baptist Church at the Mall, and the fantastic staff and people who are family. Thank you for believing in your pastor.

And now, to the most important acknowledgment of all, to my precious wife, Angie. You have shown incredible understanding, love, patience, encouragement, and have been the greatest prayer warrior to me and the best friend a man could ever have.

*P*reface: A Word from the Front Line

We are at war: the hardcore war against pornography.

Breaking free from the deadly lure of porn—this tempting and addictive evil—is a war we do not have to face alone. Men of all ages are joining this movement that shows how to make and keep a preemptive commitment to porn-free living. And we are experiencing revival as a result.

As a man, I know the shame that came with a momentary exposure to pornography as a young teen, and the power that shame once had over me. I am aware how pornographic images are ever-present and I must, as a Christian man, adjust my spiritual armor daily, and guard my eyes and mind. I can only do this by God's power.

As a senior pastor, I am aware of how pornography has leapt from printed page to high-powered digital image, pervading our culture—including the church pew and even the church pulpit. But I also know that confessing the sin of viewing pornography allows us to overcome shame, live in freedom, and share that power with other men. This is my lifetime commitment to God, my wife, my family, the church, and those we reach.

This men's book, *Our Hardcore* Commitment App, Join1MillionMen.org, *Our Hardcore Battle Plan for Wives*, *Our Hardcore Battle Plan* DVD, and associated materials are written from my heart, as I have counseled many men of all ages in my church, and I have seen how pornography seeks to destroy men, their families, and their power to serve Christ. I committed myself to studying about pornography, and I continue to examine the research that shows how porn remains in epidemic proportions—among God's people.

I not only know what God's Word says about this—but I have seen with my own eyes how this sin breaks men's fellowship with God. Pornography destroys the passion for leadership and service. It wounds Christian men, in addition to Christian women and children. Pornography negates healthy marriages and families, threatens the churches those families comprise, and worse. This evil hurts the very people God has sent us to serve—the least of these upon whom pornography purveyors prey through trafficking of humans, especially children and women.

Yet I have also witnessed how commitment to Scripture, prayer, and accountability, in Christian community, have tremendous impact against this sin. As my wife, Angie, states emphatically on our DVD—we're mad at what pornography is doing to Christians. And I would add, we're fighting mad! Having remained on the front lines of dealing with men, as well as their wives and families, and experiencing the horrible outcomes when pornography is left unaddressed, we've acquired a passion to address and to serve those in need with tried and proven weapons for healing and victory.

Freedom from pornography absolutely requires that we:
• See pornography for what it is and train ourselves to overcome this enemy.
• Resolve to remain watchful against this force.
• Make and maintain an individual commitment against pornography,
• Join forces with others in accountability to war and win against porn.

At my church, and on our Web site Join1MillionMen.org, we call this "getting on the wall." Picture this as an army with interlocking shields opposing the enemy, an impenetrable wall that connects and defends our families and church bodies as we move forward with the gospel.

Our interconnections in freedom from pornography transcend generation, culture, denomination, and particular church membership—as you will see in this movement and our materials. And while our focus in this book is on men, we know that women have a crucial role in this movement. You see that more clearly in the correlating book, *Our Hardcore Battle Plan for Wives: Winning in the War Against Pornography*.

Here and in the wives' material, we are also focusing on those who have not yet struggled. Since the average age of a boy's first exposure to pornography is between 10 and 11 years old, we are helping fathers and parents to protect sons, and their daughters.

Men who struggle with pornography—more specifically, the high percentage of those men within the church who struggle—are in a spiritual battle. This requires a spiritual movement that enlists other pastors and churches beyond the church where this movement originated. The series DVD shows some of the more than one thousand men who have gotten on the wall at our church, First Baptist Church at the Mall (FBC), in Lakeland, Florida. It also shows some of the other churches across the country who are joining the battle that began for our church in 2010, and how men are helping other men.

In the midst of preparing materials for our men at FBC, God gave us this idea. It was around Thanksgiving 2009 when I was traveling from my hometown, Fort Smith, Arkansas, after visiting with my mom, who had lost my dad earlier that year. While in a Christian bookstore there, I picked up a book by John Maxwell, *Put Your Dream to the Test.*

While reading that on the plane trip back to Tampa, I came across a statement that hit me like a ton of bricks: "If you don't quantify your dream, you will never be able to communicate it," Maxwell said. Then the Holy Spirit clearly placed on my heart, "One Million Men." Obviously that was exciting! Yet, I thought, what is the rest of that One Million Men? For the next two weeks my question to God was, But one million men what?

December 2009, God filled in the blank: 1 Million Men Porn-Free. I thought: if churches of all sizes and denominations would get involved, we could have an army of men committed to purity, and that purity could bring a powerful awakening in churches! What if one million women in churches began praying for one million men in churches to live pornography-free lives? When godly women begin praying, God-sized things happen!

That began my writing journey: man-friendly, scripturally-based, and grace-driven materials from a senior pastor's perspective. The response has been very encouraging, and the transformed lives have made the effort beyond worth it. We presented the material to FBC Lakeland in 2010, and our church will never be the same!

Our desire is expand these same Christian principles to encourage you and others, whether you are struggling with any level of viewing pornography, or whether you have from your past a pornographic image you were exposed to, as I was, that you have not yet defeated.

Even if you have never struggled with viewing pornography—I hate to tell you this—but no matter your age, you, too, are not immune from either accidentally being exposed to pornography or intentionally clicking on an image while on computer, Smartphone, or other mobile device, and finding yourself in a mental place God never wants you to go. Within mere seconds, Satan has an opportunity there to create an environment for a lust that you will have to battle.

Instead of feeling the shame and guilt of staying there, you can do something about it right now! With God's grace and strength, activated by your applying God's truth, freedom is always available. The resources you will find in this book and at our Web site designed to help you, at whatever level of struggle you are having.

What You'll Find Here

QR codes that link you to short 10- to 60-second online videos related to the book not only provide visual introductions to content. These are designed to communicate essential truths that help to illustrate the chapters.

In the three sections of this book, we'll focus first on awareness of how our enemy is perverting the healthy, good sex that God plans for men and women. We will examine the truth by focusing on empowering Scriptures and biblical principles, including Scripture study in the Book of Proverbs and other Bible passages related to awareness. We also examine Satan's counterfeit plan for sex with statistics, definitions, practices, and consequences concerning pornography.

We next include how our hardcore battle plan allows us to fight back with biblical tools already proven successful for thousands of men.

Finally, this book provides our commitment section that includes helps for men, our families, and our faith communities to implement a point-by-point follow-up plan for moment-by-moment success each day—together.

Additional material helps men and women to help their sons, providing valuable resources, including how to access therapy.

Join us! Let's begin the conversation! Let's address the issue of pornography—and develop the healthy habits we need in what is a war that we win together.

Jay Dennis, senior pastor,
First Baptist Church at the Mall, Lakeland, Florida
Join1MillionMen.org

JOIN
1 MILLION
MEN

JOIN1MILLIONMEN.ORG

Part 1

Know Our Enemy

"Have mercy on me, O God, according to your unfailing love; according to your great compassion blot out my transgressions. Wash away all my iniquity and cleanse me from my sin. For I know my transgressions, and my sin is always before me. Against you, you only, have I sinned and done what is evil in your sight. . . . Cleanse me with hyssop, and I will be clean; wash me, and I will be whiter than snow. Let me hear joy and gladness; let the bones you have crushed rejoice. Hide your face from my sins and blot out all my iniquity. Create in me a pure heart, O God, and renew a steadfast spirit within me."

—PSALM 51:1–4, 7–10 (NIV)—

1: *Shine the Light on Secrets and Sex*

"Here they are, Lord Jesus, my hidden sins. I bring them out of the secret chamber of my heart. I take them out of the darkness and expose them to Your light. Lord, You have promised You will execute Your word upon the earth, thoroughly and quickly. Oh God, thoroughly cleanse my heart; purify me quickly!"

—Christian minister and author, Francis Frangipane

The Truth

The majority of Christian men are struggling with the temptation to look at pornography. Porn has invaded the church because our men—primarily through the Internet—have allowed or even invited it into their lives. For the most part, we have left ourselves open and unprotected when it comes to the Web.

On Baylor University's Counseling Center's Web site, the following statistics should alarm everyone, especially Jesus' followers:

> It is no secret that the average man looks at pornography much more frequently than the average woman. What most people underestimate is the immensity of the problem and its effects. While the religious and moral nature of a home can have some effect on how old males are when exposed to pornography, even a very protective home is . . . frequently inadequate protection. One survey found that 91% of men raised in Christian homes, 96% of men raised in partially Christian homes, and 98% of men raised in non-Christian homes were exposed to pornography while growing up. These statistics are staggering and frightening when it comes to the emotional health of men.[1]

Here is the heart of the problem: Every man who's ever been on the Internet is at least at risk of viewing pornography. Some spend hours every day actively seeking pornography—and will lose their job and wife and family as a result. Other men may have viewed pornography once while on a business trip ten years ago and try daily to resist, though the Internet is an ever-present temptation. What we are talking about here is a wide range of people and degrees of temptation. However, pornography is a slippery slope, whatever your experience; one look can hook. And it's only through the power of the Holy Spirit that we can break free. I say *we*, because we in the church are in this together.

As a pastor, I have seen firsthand pornography's devastating effects on a man, his marriage, home, job, and his leadership within the church. When a Christian man, whether single, a husband, or a father, is viewing pornography, his passion for God and influence for God will be virtually silenced, a place where Satan wants every Christian man.

Men who love God, men who love their wives, and those who love their families and churches—who genuinely desire to do right—are prey to pornography. It seems that no church or Christian remains untouched.

True, Christians possess the power to break free from pornography. So it's not a matter of Can a man be set free from pornography? but Will that Christian man do what is necessary to live in freedom? Your awareness, planning, and commitment today could be the beginning of that wonderful experience of peace, joy, real love, and guiltlessness—a fantastic feeling!

Pastors Struggle

During the taping of the DVD for this series, we heard many Christian men reveal how they got involved with pornography, and how it devastated them.

One youth pastor explains how he lost his church ministry, injured his marriage, and almost lost it all in his involvement with porn. It has been a long hard road for him, and his wife and kids, but he has found freedom in a community of committed Christian men who are holding him accountable to be honest.

When you combine the facts that (1) many Christian men are silently struggling with this shame-based issue, and (2) many pastors are either unwilling or afraid to deal with Christians who view pornography, you have the recipe for a perfect storm within churches of all sizes and denominations.

We are beginning to see the aftermath of this moral tsunami among church leadership and members; the result of allowing pornography into their lives and the consequences when church leaders refuse to address the subject head on.

In a *Baptist Press* article, LifeWay Research president Ed Stetzer related this information from his survey of 1,000 US Protestant pastors:

> Most pastors believe pornography has adversely impacted the lives of their church members, but almost half cannot estimate what percentage of their congregation views porn.
>
> When presented with the statement, "Pornography has adversely affected the lives of our church members," the pastors responded as follows:
> - 69 percent agreed (42 percent strongly agreed; 27 percent somewhat agreed)
> - 9 percent somewhat disagreed
> - 8 percent strongly disagreed
> - 14 percent did not know or preferred not to answer.
>
> "Most pastors know pornography's poisonous effects," Stetzer said. "They've seen it destroy marriages, wreck lives and warp America's moral compass when it comes to sexuality."
>
> When asked to estimate the percentage of men in their congregations who view pornography on a weekly basis, the pastors answered as follows:
> - 62 percent said less than 10 percent
> - 24 percent said 10–24 percent
> - 10 percent said 25–49 percent
> - 4 percent said 50 percent or more
> - 43 percent were unable or unwilling to respond.[2]

Rather than deny or neglect the issue that Christian men view pornography, we need to address the issue openly—in truth and in love; with firmness and grace. Our men are ready right now, watching, and waiting for the leadership to broach the plague of pornography in the pew. Most would welcome some practical help.

You or someone you know and love is struggling with pornography. I guarantee it.

Christian Men View Pornography

I remember going through my favorite book other than the Bible, *Mere Christianity*, by C. S. Lewis. He addressed the claim made by those outside of Christ that Christians were sheltered from temptation:

> A silly idea is current that good people do not know what temptation means. This is an obvious lie. Only those who try to resist temptation know how strong it is. . . . A man who gives in to temptation after five minutes simply does not know what it would have been like an hour later. That is why bad people, in one sense, know very little about badness. They have lived a sheltered life by always giving in.

Satan, the world around us, and our sinful fleshly nature are constantly looking for and creating opportunities to do something that dishonors God and destroys our testimony and influence. The Christian has, however, the power of the Holy Spirit within, accessed through obedience and faith.

Based on my pastoral ministry through the decades, I would argue that 80 percent of men in churches are struggling with some level of viewing pornography. Many surveys are indicating that more than 50 percent of pastors are struggling with it. Covenanteyes.com provides statistical information that is increasingly staggering:

- More than 1 in 8 Web searches are for erotic content.
- 67 percent of children admit to clearing their Internet history to hide their online activity.
- 79 percent of accidental exposures to Internet porn among kids take place in the home.
- 56 percent of divorce cases involve one party having an obsessive interest in online porn.
- 29 percent of working adults accessed explicit Web sites on work computers.

Most families in the Christian church have been affected by pornography, either directly or through someone they are close to who has been adversely affected.

Satan is targeting Christian men, and the Internet is the tool available now to make the temptation more intense and appealing. Internet pornography is readily available, affordable (much of it is free), has the promise of anonymity, and it is *addictive*. No Christian home or church is unaffected. The problem will only get worse, unless Christian leaders rise up and say Enough!

Baylor University's Counseling Center's Web site informs us:

> Apparently pornography does not show bias toward one's religious affiliation or lack thereof. Some positive statistical differences exist between Christians and non-Christians. For example, Christians have a slightly later age of first exposure to pornography. However, Christians still seem to have all the same issues with pornography non-Christians experience.

Sexual Bondage Is Entrenched in the Church

Of 1,351 pastors surveyed, 54 percent had viewed Internet pornography within the last year, and 50 percent of men and 20 percent of women in the church regularly view porn.[1]

This statistic reveals the enormity of the problem. Fifty percent regularly view pornography. However, we know that basically nine out of ten, nearly every man or pastor, have had some sort of exposure to pornography in the past, or will view it in the future. Yet, if you have a pornography problem to some degree, or if you are among the 50 percent in the midst of addiction, you can still resist pornography and actively pursue freedom.

We want you to understand that you are not alone, but also know that God does not want you to stay where you are.

I also encourage those of you who have yet to meet the Lord to use this book and the practical advice that can help you with your struggles. Because, in my experience, there is no complete and lasting victory over pornography and its guilt outside of Jesus Christ. Jesus is the hope we offer, and I hope you will read page 131 about how to know Him and have His power working in your life.

CATHY AND GREG DYER

Cathy and her husband, Greg, share their testimony of Greg's deliverance from pornography in the wives' book in this series, and on the DVD, and on the *Hardcore Battle Plan* App.

Greg became captive as a young teen, and the cycle continued with him for years, entrenching pornography in his life. He was ensnared in pornography before breaking free. He describes in detail the fears and bondage that occurred before he got help.

It is important to understand this cycle of sexual bondage that is the consequence of viewing pornography. This vicious warfare will continue until addressed.

The key to experiencing freedom is to interrupt this cycle—early. Some under fire feel they cannot escape. Understanding how the bondage happens can help us to take the necessary steps to freedom. Notice first the visual and then the explanation:

How a Pornography Problem Develops

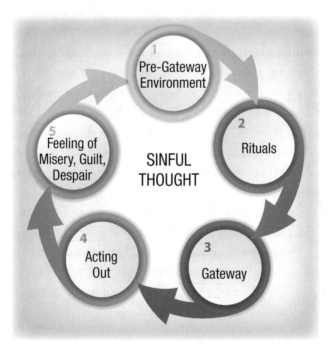

A sinful thought enters your mind. Satan will make sure that sinful thoughts bombard your mind. It only takes one sinful thought to begin the process of viewing pornography. The flesh attempts to hide the thought instead of exposing it. That "hidden" thought becomes the basis for sexual sin. According to one MSNBC/Standford/Duquesne Study, 70 percent of those who view pornography keep their habit a secret.

There is a pre-gateway environment. This is an atmosphere that creates a greater vulnerability for sexual sin to take place. That can happen more easily when a Christian is not practicing the spiritual disciplines of worship, Bible study, and prayer. Further, painful past experiences such as abuse and abandonment lead to greater vulnerability. The impact of past experiences is noteworthy.

The temptation to view pornography can be more intense if there are emotional needs created by experiences, such as rejection, broken relationships, anger, and unresolved conflicts. As well, unusual seasons of stress, lack of intimacy with your wife, past exposures to pornography (usually as a child), physical tiredness, loneliness, and those times after a defeat—or after a victory can precede the temptation. Each of these can contribute to creating an environment where sexual sin can take root.

If the issues mentioned are not addressed in a biblically consistent way, a person becomes an easier target for Satan to tempt with pornography. Some Christian men turn to pornography in an attempt to medicate the pain created by their past or by stress. Without support, they entertain sin.

Rituals kick in. A ritual is what you do to get ready to act out on your sexual stronghold—in this case, looking at pornography. "When the ritual begins, the battle is lost," according to Dr. Mark Laaser.

Rituals are different for each man, but they are usually consistent. A man will normally follow the same attitudes, actions, and choices to get to the point of viewing pornography. Ritualization happens when "the person places himself in a position in which he is ready to act out, even while consciously telling himself he is not going to view pornography again," writes Dr. Donald Hilton, Jr. in *He Restoreth My Soul.*

Gateways open. The main portal for sexual sin today is Internet pornography, although access can be gained through adult-oriented businesses, strip clubs, theaters, erotic massage parlors, sex shops, by way of cell phones, premium cable channels, cybersex, DVDs, and visiting prostitutes. A Christian man should feel conviction at this point.

Acting out occurs. This includes a wide range of activities. Often, this happens through masturbation. Acting out also includes visiting an adult-oriented business, visiting a prostitute, paying for sexual favors, cybersex activities, phone sex, or having an affair.

Once there is acting out, a Christian man is then filled with shame, guilt, despair, and unbelief that he has done such a thing. The Holy Spirit convicts. However, unless there is true repentance and accountability, the vicious cycle will continue. Some have found themselves captive in that place and escape seems hopeless. The good news is that there is a way to break through, as you will see as you progress through this book.

GREG

Greg Dyer explains how the acting out associated with his pornography use almost destroyed his family, and how a program through the church could have helped to prevent all that he and his family went through.

Pornography Destroys Good Sex

Pornography and God's standard for healthy sex are opposites. So what is the difference between healthy sex and pornography? Let's focus on what God says—and then on what pornography does:

Pornography harms;	God's way of sex brings joy.
Pornography demeans women;	God's way of sex treats women with the utmost respect and honor.
Pornography is designed to create lust;	God's way of sex is designed to bring intimacy.
Pornography focuses on physical acts only;	God's way of sex considers body, soul, and spirit.

Pornography presents unreal expectations;	God's way of sex is real, tangible, and experiential—physically, spiritually, and emotionally.
Pornography disregards the issue of sex only in marriage;	God's way of sex is reserved only for marriage—to protect, fulfill, and satisfy.
Pornography primarily focuses on bringing pleasure to the man;	God's way of sex focuses equally on meeting the needs of husband and wife.
Pornography suggests doing acts that treat women as mere sex objects;	God's way of sex always brings equal honor to both the man and the woman.
Pornography presents multiple sexual partners;	God's way of sex is exclusivity with one's spouse.

Men engaged in Join 1 Million Men recount through *Our Hardcore Battle Plan* DVD their personal stories and beliefs regarding pornography. Among them, several describe how pornography promised good things, but then delivered a deadly blow to their lives. Involvement with porn destroyed good sex, and it had horrible consequences for them. We will look at more of pornography's many negative consequences in the next chapter. Pornography is a minefield you do not want to cross.

As we study the issue of Christian men who view pornography, it is essential to come back to Scripture and to review the unchanging standard God has put in place for healthy sex. God is *not* against sex—quite the contrary. He made sex as the most wonderful gift imaginable, not just for procreation, but for pleasure without guilt and shame.

Why did God place absolute boundaries around sex? The two main reasons: to protect us from destruction, and to reflect His glory. But, as with any good gift God gives, Satan attempts to counterfeit, pervert, twist, and use what God intends for good to inflict pain and sorrow. Pornography is Satan's counterfeit to God's reality, a reality that is without guilt and shame, and Satan's design is to rob and to destroy you, your family, and ministry.

2: *Confront the Consequences*

Confronting the destructive consequences of pornography in the present will help prevent devastating effects in the future. Let's consider and remind one another of these specific consequences and effects, when we choose pornography.

A*lienates You from God.* You no longer feel close to God or experience His power. You lose the joy of your salvation. Pornography robs a Christian man of God's best gifts and opportunities. The awareness of the presence of God is forfeited the moment you choose to look at pornography.

B*linds You to the Consequences.* Pornography temporarily turns off your walk with God and your relationships with your wife, your children, and others. It blinds you to what is going to happen to you spiritually, physically, emotionally, mentally, socially, vocationally, and relationally. Only in the rearview mirror do you see the utter foolishness of viewing pornography. Satan's forces are hiding consequences and making promises our enemy never keeps.

C*reates Unrealistic Expectations.* A man begins to think this is what every woman should look like and what his relationship with his wife is to mimic. Pornography, however, is unreal. Sadly, pornography is increasingly becoming the way that young men — even Christian young men — are getting their education about sex. Real-life marriage is nothing like what is presented on Internet pornography sites.

"Pornography also produces unrealistic expectations about sex in relationships. As a man lusts after pictures of naked models, he wrongly assumes that the best kind of woman is perfectly proportioned and offers constant pleasure.

Lust classifies a woman as a sex object who should fulfill a man's selfish desires, instead of a precious person to be loved sacrificially," Rob Eagar explains in his article, "Fooled by Fantasy," posted on Growthtrac.com.

*D*istorts Your View of Sex. Pornography makes you believe that sex is solely for the pleasure of a man and that women are simply objects to be used rather than God's creations to be honored and respected. Dr. Michael Bader, author of *Male Sexuality*, shares that, in his experience as a counselor, "the two most passionate objections women raise concerning pornography are (a) that men want their real-life partners to look like porn stars and do what porn stars do, and (b) that pornography reflects the male wish that women put their bodies and sexuality at the service of men. Both assumptions make women feel devalued."

*E*nough Is Never Enough. Pornography has an escalating effect. Like taking an addictive drug, you need more and more to satisfy the lust. It takes you further down a destructive path and further away from peace, joy, and healthy relationships. That is why a man who starts out looking at a pornographic image, over time, can begin to desire those images and activities that were once appalling to him.

William M. Struthers of Wheaton College explains how porn works in his book, *Wired for Intimacy: How Pornography Hijacks the Male Brain*, "If I take the same dose of a drug over and over and my body begins to tolerate it, I will need to take a higher dose of the drug in order for it to have the same effect that it did with a lower dose the first time."

> Something about pornography pulls and pushes at the male soul. The pull is easy to identify. The naked female form can be hypnotizing. A woman's willingness to participate in a sexual act or expose her nakedness is alluring to men. The awareness of one's own sexuality, the longing to know, to experience something as good wells up from deep within. An image begins to pick up steam the longer we look upon it. It gains momentum and can reach a point where it feels like a tractor-trailer rolling downhill with no brakes.

Albert Mohler explains further in his review of this "hijacking" at Crosswalk .com:

> Pornography is "visually magnetic" to the male brain. Enough is never enough. The experience of viewing pornography and acting out on it creates a demand in the brain for more and more, just to achieve the same level of pleasure in the brain.

Freedom Is Replaced by Addiction. When pornography is added to your mind, you cannot erase or undo what you chose. You can become enslaved to your sinful thoughts, which leads to sinful actions. Pornography's power to change you cannot be overstated.

Guilt Comes. A Christian man who views pornography brings guilt and shame into his life, but the power of shame and guilt is not enough to stop him from going back. As a Christian, you possess the power to overcome this bondage, but it will not be easy. The desire to love and obey God, not the desire to be guilt free, is the most powerful motivation to live a pornography-free life.

Healthy Sexuality Is Contradicted. Godly, healthy sex is married sex only—loving sex and unselfish sex. Pornography presents sexual activity that does not include God.

Isolates You. Pornography makes you feel you are all alone and are the only one who struggles with it. The nature of pornography brings a sense of loneliness and shame to a Christian man. He doesn't want to tell anyone about his problem because he is so filled with guilt and the feeling that no one else battles with this issue. It is Satan's way of keeping a Christian man quiet and preventing him from being the spiritual leader in his home and church.

Jeopardizes Your Relationships. Pornography damages your marriage (or future marriage), your witness for Jesus Christ, and everything else in your life that is important to you. You put it all on the line for pornography. Every Christian man would surely say, "Pornography is not worth it!" But the four-fold nature of pornography—availability, anonymity, affordability, and addictiveness—creates a powerful pull toward looking and becoming captive.

*K*eeps You in a Self-Destructive Cycle. It may appear to medicate the pain in your life, but it only adds to the pain with more pain. Pornography leads you to do things you never thought you would do.

"Sin will take you farther than you want to go, keep you longer than you want to stay, and cost you more than you want to pay" (author unknown).

*L*ust. Pornography plants the seeds of sexual sinful lust, which leads to sexual sinful actions. What you think about the most, you will eventually act upon. Viewing pornography moves you one step closer to acting out what you have seen. Dr. Pat Love wrote in *"Is MySpace YourSpace?*, Yourtango.com:

> Viewing sexual stimulation recalibrates your sexual set point; that is, once your mind forms a picture or has a new sexual experience, this becomes the norm. To get another thrill, you need something even more exciting. This is how porn use can destroy your interest and attraction for your mate. Repeated pornography use numbs normal sexual drives and deadens your desire for a real person.
>
> In addition, bizarre as it may seem, the more shame you feel about your guilty pleasures—the more you resent your partner! We don't like people who remind us of our bad behavior. When you violate the lines of your own commitment and values, you actually end up looking for faults in your partner to alleviate your guilt. "Well, if she were more (fill in the blank), I wouldn't be doing this." And the guiltier you feel, the more vulnerable you become to the escape of a sexual high.
>
> Millions of people are currently caught in the excitement cycle of porn use or an affair, either online or face to face. And if you think it will stop where it is, research proves you very, very wrong. Relationships which begin in cyberspace eventually meet face to face in some way, shape, or form.

*M*asks Your Real Wound. Men often use pornography to cover up an old hurt, but porn just makes things worse. Pornography is a medication that many men, including Christians, are turning to in an effort to find excitement, relief, and release. However, viewing pornography only adds to the pain, the grief, and the problems.

***N**ever a Neutral Experience.* You cannot look at porn and not be affected by it. That experience is always inconsistent with God's Word. Pornography is designed to illicit a response, and it always gets one. For the Christian man, that response cannot be holy.

***O**bjectifies Women.* It makes the woman a sexual object. Porn hijacks a man's ability to see an older woman as a mother figure, a same-aged woman as a sister figure, and a younger woman as a daughter figure. Pornography turns women into objects that serve a man's selfish desires, an attitude to which the Bible is diametrically opposed.

***P**leasure Is Very Short-Lived.* Then come the long-term guilt and pain. Satan focuses on that moment of pleasure when he is tempting you to look at pornography; however, that short moment is immediately followed by long-lasting guilt, shame, and pain.

***Q**uitting Becomes a Lifelong Struggle.* Once you allow porn in, you begin a raging battle with Satan and with your flesh that wants to keep looking. That mental battle will always be there. This is a winnable battle, but a daily battle. The more that pornography is allowed into your mind, the greater the life-time battle will be. To paraphrase a famous Mark Twain quit-smoking quote, applying it to pornography addiction: "It's easy to quit. I've done it hundreds of times." The addictive nature of pornography makes it extremely difficult to quit simply.

***R**emains Imbedded in Your Mind.* Satan replays that porn image in your mind to create a cycle of sinful lust and to drive you back to its prison. You become bound to an image, not a person. Similar to a photo that's forever posted in cyberspace, once something is in your mind, you have to deal with it forever.

Shame Enters Your Life. Guilt is feeling badly for something you have done; shame, however, is based on feeling badly about who you *are*. Pornography brings shame. Satan always brings shame. God never brings shame.

Trust Is Broken. The people you love and respect the most won't ever see you the same. Pornography betrays trust, especially with your wife and those in your sphere of influence. Trust takes years to build and can be lost with one click.

Unlocks the Door to Sexual Sin. Porn is a portal, a gateway that leads to nothing good and everything painful, such as compulsive masturbation, affairs, visiting adult-oriented businesses, paying for sex, perverted sexual practices, and other sexual abuse.

Violates Women. How? You are putting your stamp of approval on an industry that degrades and dehumanizes women. Porn harms women. A Christian must never be part of something that injures women.

Morality in Media (MIM) is a national, interfaith organization formed to combat pornography and promote decency in the media. MIM believes that an increase in pornography is linked to the increase in violence against women.

In this *Christian Post* article, "Pornography Harms Women, Invades the Church," Amanda Winkler shared:

> Dawn Hawkins, Morality in Media's executive director, says that the kind of videos the porn industry produces has grown more violent due to its popularity among consumers.
>
> "Spousal violence is also one of our greatest concerns—the husband consuming violent porn and then living out the pornographic scenes in his marriage," said Hawkins. "It's destroying families. Children are becoming a lot more involved."
>
> Patrick Trueman, president of Morality in Media, agrees with Dawkins and told *Catholic News* that when men view violent porn there is not only an increase in violent behavior but sex trafficking as well. Men who view pornography see sex as "hiring prostitutes."

Trueman said, "Internet pornography consumers are essentially training their brains to demand violence, because the images available are unimaginably depraved and violent. By not putting a stop to this illegal pornography available on the Internet, our country is creating a culture of violence for today's woman."

*W*andering Eyes. Pornography places a lens on your eyes, encouraging a lustful look toward women. Your eyes become, as Pamela Paul suggests in the title of her book, *Pornified*.

*EX*tinguishes Truth. Pornography promotes lying. You lie to others, you lie to God, and you lie to yourself. You lie more to cover up past lies. You start to live a lie.

*Y*okes You to an Image. You become bound to the image, instead of to the woman in your life.

*Z*ips Your Lips. Pornography silences your mouth and prevents you from worshipping God, sharing your story of salvation, and encouraging your brothers in Christ toward holy living.

Consequences on Women

A Christian man's viewing of porn has detrimental and long-lasting effects on the woman in his life, whether she's a girlfriend, fiancée, or wife. Christian men must consider these consequences *before* they look at porn, and they must understand what she will experience *after* they've looked. Viewing porn never has a neutral affect. It always has a detrimental effect. If a man is in the habit of looking at pornography, it will not remain hidden. Here are 26 consequences on the woman when a man chooses to view pornography.

*A*llows a Third Party. You, the woman in your life, and pornography—the only third party in your relationship should be Jesus Christ! The man begins to focus more on the pornographic image in his mind rather than on his lady.

*B*reaks Her Heart. You wound the one God gave you to protect. This is so avoidable. Your viewing of pornography betrays her on every level—physically, emotionally, mentally, and relationally.

*C*reates Insecurity Within Her. She feels she can never measure up. Her first thought will probably be, "Why aren't I enough for him?"

*D*ivorce Becomes a Real Possibility in Her Mind. The *D* word now enters the picture. "At the 2003 meeting of the American Academy of Matrimonial Lawyers, a gathering of the nation's divorce lawyers, attendees revealed that 58% of their divorces were a result of a spouse's looking at excessive amounts of pornography online").[1]

*E*motionally Attacks Her. Pornography traumatizes her in her most vulnerable places. Old wounds become fresh again. She is now wondering what is wrong with her.

*F*orgetting What Happened Will Never Happen. She will always remember. Your viewing of pornography will leave a permanent emotional scar. You betrayed her by looking at another woman, even if it was just an image. That thought will always be in the back of her mind. The sense of betrayal is real.

*G*uilt Invades Her Heart. Pornography makes her feel like she has done something wrong, even though *you* are the guilty party. Satan uses your unwise choices to make her wonder if she has done something wrong or if she could have done more to meet your needs.

*H*ealing Is a Long Process for Her. Simply saying, "I'm sorry and I will never do it again," is only the beginning of a long healing process. Trust has been broken. Healing is possible through Jesus Christ and through repentance and accountability; however, healing will take much time and is a painful process.

*I*ntimacy Is Shattered. That deep connection she desires with you has been destroyed for the moment. She now understands why the intimacy was missing before. You replaced her with pornography. You robbed the focus on her and gave it to an image.

Professors Dolf Zillmann and Jennings Bryant, in the *Journal of Applied Social Psychology*, have found that "repeated exposure to pornography results in (1) a decreased satisfaction with one's sexual partner, with the partner's sexuality, and with the partner's sexual curiosity, (2) a decrease in the valuation of faithfulness, and (3) a major increase in the importance of sex without attachment."

*J*ealousy Is Validated. She has been competing with a pornographic image. Of course she is going to feel jealous. She realizes that she cannot compete with or measure up to what you have seen in pornography, and she knows she never will.

*K*now That Pornography Has Robbed Her. It has taken away her ability to say, "My man is not like that. He doesn't look at pornography. I don't ever have to worry about that." Your lady wants to be able to say that. As a Christian man, you should have this testimony, but that has now been shattered. You can begin today to rebuild that testimony.

*L*ust. Your desire for someone else — in an image — has replaced your desire for her, and she knows it. Your lady feels replaced, and she has every right to feel that way. Rather than pursuing her and intimacy with her, you're pursuing what you saw on a computer screen.

Dr. Patrick F. Fagan, director of the Center for Marriage and Religion, Family Research Council, has reported, "Married men who are involved in pornography feel less satisfied with their conjugal relations and less emotionally attached to their wives. Wives notice and are upset by the difference" (The Effects of Pornography on Individuals, Marriage, Family and Community, December 2009).

Jennifer Schneider researched Internet porn and found, in *Sexual Addiction and Compulsivity: Effects of Cybersex Addiction on the Family*, that wives began "feeling sexually inadequate or feeling unattractive and even ugly" when they realized their husbands were viewing pornography.

***M**akes You a Stranger.* Viewing pornography creates within you an emotional distance from the woman in your life, the very opposite of what God designed.

Robert Jensen, in his book *Getting Off: Pornography and the End of Masculinity,* said,

> In my experience, which is also the experience of many men I've talked to over the years, we feel ourselves go emotionally numb when viewing pornography and masturbating, what in common parlance might be called a state of being checked out.

***N**eglects Her Needs.* You were not thinking of your wife when you viewed pornography. You only focused on your needs, something that runs contrary to God's role for you as the spiritual leader of your home. The Bible teaches that you put your wife and her needs above your own. You failed to do that when you chose to look at porn. If you were thinking about your wife, you would never have looked at pornography.

***O**pens the Door to Satan.* Pornography invites Satan into your home. It is one of Satan's portals. Pornography is a gateway that the enemy is using to work in your marriage and family. You have put out a welcome mat for him to work, something that no Christian husband desires to do.

***P**otential Embarrassment.* She will wonder, *Who else knows? What do they know? What if they find out?* This is a real concern on her mind.

***Q**uestions Raised.* Your wife will wonder if all you did was look at pornography. She will now wonder if you have had a real-time affair, or if you have at least considered one. You cannot view pornography without thinking about that possibility.

***R**ealizes Your Mind Was Elsewhere.* When you have sex with your wife, she knows that your mind is not fully focused on her. It is thinking about an image with which she cannot compete. True intimacy focuses on giving yourself totally to your wife, meeting her needs.

Security Is Sacrificed. Your wife needs to have the feeling in her heart that you are there for her. A Christian wife finds freedom in the security of her husband's faithfulness. Your viewing of pornography has damaged that security, because you have acted unfaithfully.

Trust Has Been Broken. And it is extremely difficult to ever get it back. In the back of her mind she will always wonder if you are looking at pornography again. A great marriage demands trust. If you have viewed pornography, be honest with your wife, seek her forgiveness, and let her know that the passion of your life will be to rebuild that trust you have broken.

Unfaithfulness Has Become Real. Your wife views your pornography issue as unfaithfulness to your marriage vows, even if you did not have a real-time affair. The feeling of betrayal is real to your wife. She will wonder if you have considered having a physical affair. She will wonder about the women you work with, the women you are around.

Victimizes Your Wife. Your viewing of pornography makes her feel rejected by you. You chose something else over her. You knew how this would make her feel, yet you chose pornography anyway. She has become a victim.

Worries Her About Her Children. What if your children find the pornography that you have viewed? What will it do to their minds and hearts? That is a legitimate concern. Mark it down. They will find your pornography!

EXasperates Her. Pornography gives anger an invitation into her heart. Her anger was triggered by something you did that could have been avoided. She now has to deal with temptations to sin in her own life because of the anger and unforgiveness that will knock on the door of her heart.

Years. That's what it will take for her to fully believe you and trust you again, *after* you repent and begin doing the right thing. Although the Lord can help you repair the damage, there is no quick fix for the consequences of pornography. It usually requires many years and depends on how deeply you delved into it. Begin today the journey back to trust.

*Z*ero *Respect.* A Christian man who views pornography has basically said to the woman in his life, "I don't respect you." Respect is earned through action. This action has communicated effectively the message that respect for her was not a priority for you.

As a Christian, as you read these 26 consequences, you are probably feeling a heavy sense of conviction by the Holy Spirit. For you to experience freedom, you first have to see the level of hurt that pornography causes God and His daughters. Truth does set you free; however, truth first has to be admitted before a man can move forward.

The truth is that the 26 effects mentioned above are what your viewing of porn has done (or will do) to women. If you have not viewed pornography, these 26 reasons reveal why you should not. If you have viewed pornography, it is time to come clean and make some *radical* changes before you go any further. Seeing how pornography is addressed in the Bible, through God's eyes, is the next step.

3: *V*iew Pornography Through God's Eyes

With the prevalence of Internet pornography and other sexualized media, many husbands have gotten it twisted when it comes to sexual relations with their wives. And those yet to marry have corrupt ideas about what to expect from a fiancée during the engagement period, and what to expect in the future with a wife.

Pornography stimulates men to ask their wives to do self-centered sexual acts, with the man thinking only of himself. They may even request acts that are uncomfortable for and demeaning to women.

Let's clarify, with a biblical lens, what is acceptable and unacceptable when it comes to sexual practices. If you stay within God-ordained boundaries, you can expect a fulfilling sex life where your needs are met. If you go outside God's boundaries, you've entered your enemy's territory.

A Scripture passage that concisely gives that standard is 1 Corinthians 7:1–5, where the apostle Paul addresses marriage, singleness, and the physical aspects of marriage with the Corinthian Christians.

> *Now concerning the things about which you wrote, it is good for a man not to touch a woman. But because of immoralities, each man is to have his own wife, and each woman is to have her own husband. The husband must fulfill his duty to his wife, and likewise also the wife to her husband. The wife does not have authority over her own body, but the husband does; and likewise also the husband does not have authority over his own body, but the wife does. Stop depriving one another, except by agreement for a time, so that you may devote yourselves to prayer, and come together again so that Satan will not tempt you because of your lack of self-control.*

From those verses we can identify these four principles of healthy, acceptable sex and demonstrate the stark contrast between God's way and pornography:

1. Healthy Sex Is Married Sex

> *But because of immoralities, each man is to have his own wife, and each woman is to have her own husband* (1 Corinthians 7:2).

Love is not the boundary for sex, marriage is—and only marriage. The media most often portrays sex outside of marriage as exciting and adventurous, while sex within marriage is portrayed as boring, dull, and humdrum—just the opposite of God's reality. This is underscored by the following 2008 report from the Parents Television Council:

> Sex in the context of marriage is either nonexistent on primetime broadcast television, or is depicted as a burdensome rather than as an expression of love and commitment. By contrast, extramarital or adulterous sexual relationships are depicted with greater frequency, and overwhelmingly as a positive experience. Across the broadcast networks, verbal references to nonmarital sex outnumbered references to sex in the context of marriage by nearly 3 to 1; and scenes depicting or implying sex between nonmarried partners outnumbered scenes depicting or implying sex between married partners by a ratio of nearly 4 to 1.

Pornography puts absolutely no credence on sex in marriage. The portrayal on porn sites is most often between unmarried people. And as has been mentioned and documented thoroughly, many of these are trafficked peoples. Others are desperate individuals who are preying on others for their own gain, with complete disregard for Jesus Christ and His followers.

Pornography promotes sex outside of marriage. So if you view pornography, you are putting your stamp of approval on sex outside of marriage. Dr. Walt Larimore, reporting in a survey at imom.com, shows us that the greatest and most satisfying sexual experience is between a man and his wife within the boundaries of marriage.

2. Healthy Sex Is Regular Sex

> *Stop depriving one another, except by agreement for a time, so that*
> *you may devote yourselves to prayer, and come together again so*
> *that Satan will not tempt you because of your lack of self-control*
> (1 Corinthians 7:5).

God tells husbands and wives to have sex on a regular basis. Sex is never to be used as a reward or punishment. If this is happening, seek wise counsel from a Christian therapist to help you work through your issues. Also, the only time a married couple should refrain from regular sex is for the purpose of praying for a short time and a specific reason. An absence of regular sex will create opportunities for temptation, something Satan fully understands.

Abstaining from sex is permissible for a period of time if both husband and wife agree to it, and for the purposes of prayer and fasting—but only for such times. Coming back together physically is essential. Satan has an ingenious way of tempting us when we least expect it. A strong, consistent sex life becomes a magnet that keeps both husband and wife drawn back to each other. I am not suggesting that if you have a great sex life you will never be tempted to look at pornography, but it is a strong deterrent from many temptations. Men, if you are struggling with pornography, you can in no way point the blame at your wife, regardless of how much or how little sex you have with her. Choosing to view pornography is a decision of which you are totally responsible.

Those who are single or choose to remain single must wrestle with Scripture Christian men committed to rejecting porn for Christ's sake and their own good must dwell on what God tells them. There is no substitute for this. They must be in fellowship with other men who have achieved some victory in Christ. What does that look like? That is men going to the Scriptures to transform and renew their minds. Looking at the life of Jesus Christ is a wonderful place to start. Another example of a godly man who resisted evil and who accomplished great things for God is the Apostle Paul.

3. Healthy Sex Is Unselfish Sex

Pornography focuses on self-centeredness, especially a man's desires. The Bible presents an entirely selfless ideal of sex in the marriage relationships.

The husband must fulfill his duty to his wife, and likewise also the wife to her husband. The wife does not have authority over her own body, but the husband does; and likewise also the husband does not have authority over his own body, but the wife does (1 Corinthians 7:3–4).

Duty means a debt, a responsibility. It means to give sexual satisfaction to each other. In other words, you are responsible to meet each other's needs sexually. Husbands and wives have equal rights when it comes to sex.

"Stop depriving" (7:5) means don't rob each other, don't keep a distance, don't withhold.

Paul teaches that the husband and wife release the authority of their bodies over to each other. Within marriage, couples can find everything they need to fulfill their sexual needs. Married couples owe each other sexual happiness. The goal of sex between husband and wife is mutual pleasure, which is not accomplished by seeking self-satisfaction first. This is the opposite of pornography's portrayal.

4. Healthy Sex Is Loving Sex

Loving refers to gentleness, tenderness, patience, and kindness toward your marriage partner in the sexual experience. Sex is not demanded, it is given.

Rights and responsibilities to each other are different from demanding from each other. Healthy sex does not insist that the marriage partner do things that are uncomfortable emotionally, spiritually, or physically. There should be an agreement between the two regarding what is acceptable and within the boundaries of comfort and security. If a woman is uncomfortable with certain aspects or acts of sex, she should communicate that to her husband, and the husband should respect that.

Again, pornography often presents sexual acts that are demeaning, uncomfortable, unsafe, unhealthy, and designed only to meet the desires of the man. This is not God's way.

The study, "The Social Costs of Pornography," noted eight specific negative findings concerning porn. The third one states that pornography can harm women especially, whether these women are girlfriends or wives of the persons viewing the pornography. The women can be harmed even when they are consuming it themselves, because pornography shapes what any culture expects—and in this case, expects about female sexual behavior. We must also realize that the women and even children used by pornography often are abused as well as those enslaved and trafficked by persons profiting from this prevalent evil.[1]

That finding alone should cause any Christian man to never support that industry by viewing pornography.

Each couple must decide for themselves in the Spirit of Jesus what is appropriate for them—though pornography is never appropriate. There should be no violation of each other's comfort zones or consciences. Viewing pornography together is inviting a third person into your marriage and creates sinful lust. This absolutely should not be allowed.

Should married couples be creative? Yes, but not at the expense of making either feel uncomfortable.

Pornography wrecks intimacy in a marriage, and relegates the 3D relationship—body, soul, and spirit—to one dimension only: the physical aspect. And that's not enough. If you're using your emotional reserves on someone not your spouse at the expense of your spouse, that's infidelity. Consider *Webster's* definition of *unfaithful*: "not faithful: not adhering to vows, allegiance, or duty." Nowhere does it state that unfaithfulness or infidelity is tied to a physical act.

Pornography does not portray God's best, God's way to health and happiness in marriage. There is nothing about pornography that will add anything good or positive to your marriage. It will add temptation, lust, and insecurity. Anything inconsistent with the will of God could never enhance your marriage.

The more you understand about how pornography can trap a Christian man and place him in spiritual and emotional bondage, the more prepared you will be to conquer it. If you are aware of the path that leads you to giving into the temptation to view pornography, you can build in safeguards to conquer this fatal attraction.

Consider the four previous principles with your accountability group.

The Word on Defile

The writer of Hebrews says, "Marriage is to be held in honor among all, and the marriage bed is to be undefiled; for fornicators and adulterers God will judge" (13:4).

The word *defile* has the idea of "soiling" or "impurity." A husband's viewing of pornography is one way the Christian marriage bed is being defiled today. To bring that into the marriage relationship betrays his marriage vows and betrays his being the spiritual leader of his home.

God does not want you to compare what you have in your marriage with what is portrayed in an unreal way in an ungodly, pornographic, perverted scene. Bringing any kind of pornography into your home dishonors Christian marriage and dishonors your wife, as it negates your role as the spiritual leader and protector of your wife and home.

Consider the testimonies of others who are recovering from defiling their marriages. Their stories are teaching us the ways to avoid the disastrous consequences of continuing in pornography. You'll find them available though your men's group, pastor, app, and online at Join1MillionMen.org.

One Woman's Reaction

When you study what Jesus said in Matthew 5:28, the problem becomes clearer. "But I say to you that everyone who looks at a woman with lust for her has already committed adultery with her in his heart."

So can a man view pornography and not feel lust in his heart? The answer is an obvious no. Any man who views pornography is committing adultery in his heart against his wife and sinning against God. Are the consequences the same? History and experience tell us that, over time, what we dwell on we tend to act on.

Viewing pornography opens the door to the physical act of adultery. Arguing otherwise is futile. Your wife believes that your viewing of pornography is committing adultery. It is a betrayal and attacks the wife at the very core of one of her greatest needs from her husband—the need for security. When she discovers he has been looking at pornography, that sense of security is undermined. Coauthor of the women's book, Cathy Dyer, expresses this from her personal experience:

> Obviously if you discover your husband has been viewing pornography you feel betrayed, hurt, angry, embarrassed, and violated. Trust has been broken. You feel devalued and disrespected. Insecurity makes you wonder "Why aren't I enough for him?" although you are not

the reason he looked at pornography. You are probably beginning to connect the dots as to why your husband seemed so distant, almost like a stranger at times. You feel embarrassed and rejected.

You worry that if your husband looked at pornography, what else has he done? If you have children you worry that they may have discovered it too? A thousand questions and emotions stir in your mind and heart. You wonder what or who was on his mind when you were having sex.

Things are beginning to make more sense now as to why your husband went into sexual overdrive wanting more sex or the opposite, a seeming disinterest in sex. Perhaps you now understand why your husband asked you to do things that were not comfortable for you. You wonder if he is looking at other women or even if he has had an affair. No doubt you feel fear about the future and have many questions about the past. When did your husband start looking at porn? How often did he view it? Does he truly love you? Why did he feel a need to find sexual excitement outside of your relationship?

Life as you knew it has changed because of your husband's choice. How committed is he to this marriage? What do you do now? How do you go forward from this point? Should you demand your husband leave? Should you go to marriage counseling? Should you demand your husband go to counseling, join a support group, and get into an accountability group? These are all issues that need to be addressed.

4: *T*ake Another Look at God's Word

Persons ever having an extramarital affair were 3.18 times more apt to have used cyberporn than ones who had lacked affairs.[1]

—Steven Stack, Ira Wasserman, and Roger Kern, "Adult Social Bonds and Use of Internet Pornography," *Social Science Quarterly*

First read Proverbs 7 below in its entirety from this contemporary translation of the Bible by Eugene Petersen: *The Message*. Then we will look at other Scripture versions as we study the territory God says His people are to avoid:

Proverbs 7 Sounds the Warning

> Dear friend, do what I tell you;
>   treasure my careful instructions.
> Do what I say and you'll live well
>   My teaching is as precious as your eyesight—guard it!
> Write it out on the back of your hands;
>   etch it on the chambers of your heart.
> Talk to Wisdom as to a sister
>   Treat Insight as your companion.
> They'll be with you to fend off the Temptress—
>   that smooth-talking, honey-tongued Seductress.
>
> As I stood at the window of my house
>   looking out through the shutters,
> Watching the mindless crowd stroll by,
>   I spotted a young man without any sense

Arriving at the corner of the street where she lived,
    then turning up the path to her house.
It was dusk, the evening coming on,
    the darkness thickening into night.
Just then, a woman met him —
    she'd been lying in wait for him, dressed to seduce him.
Brazen and brash she was,
    restless and roaming, never at home,
Walking the streets, loitering in the mall,
    hanging out at every corner in town.

She threw her arms around him and kissed him,
    boldly took his arm and said,
I've got all the makings for a feast —
    today I made my offerings, my vows are all paid,
So now I've come to find you,
    hoping to catch sight of your face — and here you are!
I've spread fresh, clean sheets on my bed,
    colorful imported linens.
My bed is aromatic with spices
    and exotic fragrances.
Come, let's make love all night,
    spend the night in ecstatic lovemaking!
My husband's not home; he's away on business,
    and he won't be back for a month."

Soon she has him eating out of her hand,
    bewitched by her honeyed speech.
Before you know it, he's trotting behind her,
    like a calf led to the butcher shop,
Like a stag lured into ambush
    and then shot with an arrow,
Like a bird flying into a net
    not knowing that its flying life is over.

So, friends, listen to me,
take these words of mine most seriously.
Don't fool around with a woman like that;
don't even stroll through her neighborhood.
Countless victims come under her spell;
she's the death of many a poor man.
She runs a halfway house to hell,
fits you out with a shroud and a coffin.

Like this woman in the story, pornography leads to adultery, emotional or physical. Not only that, Peterson's interpretation is that "it's a halfway house to hell." It's a deadly lure in an all-out war against our lives. Let's take a closer look together at God's Word. Regardless of your Bible version, illicit sexual activity—and that's clearly what pornography is—leads you down the same dark road.

PORNOGRAPHY'S ARSENAL

As we continue examining Proverbs 7, we will use the letter *A* in each point to communicate the message of a Christian man's battle with the seductive temptation of pornography, so we can clearly discern our enemy's tactics. Questions pertaining to each point can be found at the end of the chapter.

The Adulteress Arrives

That they may keep you from an adulteress,
From the foreigner who flatters with her words (Proverbs 7:5).

This woman is someone with whom the young man is not married. That makes him an adulterer. So, is Internet porn adultery? The answer is an absolute Yes! Internet pornography invites you to be unfaithful with your eyes, your mind, and your heart. It is cheating—first on God, and, if you're married or engaged, on your wife or fiancée.

I'll take it another step: a single man who hasn't yet met his wife-to-be is still committing adultery against her when he views pornography and allows his mind to record images of other women. An adulteress encourages and invites sexual unfaithfulness, which is anything outside of God's will for us, as we studied in week 1.

You are focusing on another woman, not on your wife. You are lusting after someone you are not married to, something Jesus clearly speaks to us about: "But I say, anyone who even looks at a woman with lust has already committed adultery with her in his heart" (Matthew 5:28 NLT).

Beatriz Mileham's dissertation at the University of Florida revealed that 83 percent of spouses who had cybersex didn't consider it to be cheating. Speaking of online sex, Mileham believes "the Internet will soon become the most common form of infidelity, if it isn't already."

> Viewing pornography is committing adultery—virtual adultery, but adultery just the same. Your wife, fiancée, or girlfriend feels the same sense of betrayal she would feel if you had a real-time physical or emotional affair.[2]

Let's examine further the arsenal that awaits those who enter pornography's territory.

The Adulteress Affirms

> *Who flatters with her words* (Proverbs 7:5).

Men have a need for affirmation, to feel admired and respected. Pornography flatters you. It tells you, I'm here for you, for your pleasure, to meet your sexual needs. Your wife may not be meeting all your sexual needs, but I will. Your wife may not do the things sexually you want her to do, but I will—anything goes.

> *I was due to offer peace offerings;*
> *Today I have paid my vows.*
> *Therefore I have come out to meet you,*
> *To seek your presence earnestly, and I have found you"*
> (Proverbs 7:14–15).

In other words, *What took you so long?* Pornography will slay you with guilt and shame when it's over, but before you act out (primarily through masturbation), it is very affirming. After masturbation, reality sets in, and then guilt, shame, and disbelief emerge.

You can see that if a man's wife is not affirming him, viewing porn can be a real temptation. That is no excuse, but it is something every man needs from his wife—and something that is earned.

There is a certain atmosphere that takes place leading up to viewing Internet pornography. It's the zone a Christian man can get into, leading up to temptation. It can be the time, location, feelings, thoughts leading up to when you are confronted with temptation. Maybe you are . . .

- ❑ Stressed out
- ❑ Lonely
- ❑ Tired
- ❑ Depleted physically
- ❑ Drained emotionally
- ❑ In an unhappy marriage
- ❑ Having a bad day
- ❑ Experiencing pain
- ❑ In a strained relationship
- ❑ Feeling insecure

When you combine these circumstances with the reality that you have not been in God's Word, in prayer, in accountability, nor in passionate pursuit of God's holiness, you have the conditions for a perfect storm.

Satan whispers to you, *You need something to make you happy. The quickest way is to get online.* Gentlemen, this is when and where you will either win this battle or lose it.

Notice this young man was "naive" in Proverbs 7:7. The definition implies a person who is open to something. Temptation knocks; you are now considering opening the door. You haven't opened the door or walked through it yet, but you are thinking about it. What if? Curiosity makes you wonder what's it like?

Another way to look at this is through the word *rituals*—the processes you go through to get to the point of viewing porn. You don't just end up one day in front of your computer screen searching for pornography. You took specific steps to get to that place. Even though you told yourself, *I won't look at porn again,* you placed yourself in a position where you are ready to act out. If you want to get free and experience victory, you have to put roadblocks in front of the rituals.

An example of a ritual would be thinking about how you are going to sit down at your computer when no one is around. You think about when, how, and where you will look at pornography. You begin to plan the scenario. It's what the Bible calls making provision for the flesh. "But put on the Lord Jesus Christ, and make no provision for the flesh in regard to its lusts" (Romans 13:14). Bill Hybels writes in *Tender Love:*

> Sexual sin doesn't just happen. It almost always is the result of a process of nurturing temptation. When people (with whom we feel a sexual chemistry) are placed in our lives, our natural inclination is to run from or nurture temptation. Both tacks will likely lead to sexual sin.

Always Available

Passing through the street near her corner;
And he takes the way to her house (Proverbs 7:8).

The man in the story is young, but the lesson applies to a man of any age. Men, I believe men that you will struggle with lust until you get to heaven. This man, however, is putting himself in the place where he will be tempted. Where is that place for you as far as pornography is concerned? It is at work? At home? In a hotel room? When traveling? When everyone else is asleep? When no one else is around?

Notice she comes to meet this man, who is open to being tempted. Temptation is always faithful! You can count on it. When you have even the slightest consideration or curiosity, temptation will be there to help you. The fact that you know that pornography is available, morning, noon, and night, and anytime in between, can be a real problem. There is never a CLOSED sign on Internet pornography.

I could quote statistics on the vast number of pornographic Web sites that are available, but the issue is, you know pornography is always there. People may let you down; but pornography will always be available.

> She is now in the streets, now in the squares.
> And lurks by every corner (Proverbs 7:12).

Everywhere you look, there is something sexual—billboards, cleavage, the checkout stand, TV, scantily dressed women in catalogs, those sexual pre-scription ads, ads in magazines and papers and online banners, and even in cartoons! Nearly everything is becoming sexualized and assaults a man's mind. The availability of pornography increases the temptation, even for a Christian man.

"Rule 34" is very popular in Internet circles. *Urban Dictionary*'s definition is: "Pornography or sexually related material exists for any conceivable subject." It truly is available always.

Anonymity Promised

> In the twilight, in the evening,
> In the middle of the night and in the darkness (Proverbs 7:9).

> For my husband is not at home,
> He has gone on a long journey;
> He has taken a bag of money with him,
> At the full moon he will come home (19–20).

The picture is of something hidden, a symbol of secrecy. The adulteress (or immoral woman) is saying exactly what Internet pornography says to you, *Nobody will ever know. It's a secret.*

A secret possesses the power to place a person in captivity. The idea that pornography allows you to view the images with anonymity adds to the power of the temptation. *If no one will ever know, then I can get by with it* becomes part of the trap.

However, listen to what the Bible says: "For the time is coming when everything that is covered will be revealed, and all that is secret will be made known to all" (Matthew 10:26 NLT).

Here is the reality. You will be found out. It's only a matter of time. Sin makes you sloppy and stupid. You will slip up. Your wife will find it. Your kids will find it. You will forget. You will slip up. You will be discovered. It's a stress you don't need and don't have to have.

Absolutely Appealing to the Eye

Dressed as a harlot and cunning of heart (Proverbs 7:10).

Like the adulteress, Internet pornography is specifically designed to appeal to a man's eyes. Men are hardwired to be visually stimulated. Every image is designed to avert a man's eyes toward porn instead of toward what is most important to him.

With her many persuasions she entices him;
With her flattering lips she seduces him (Proverbs 7:21).

The adulteress is deceptive and cunning of heart. Internet porn lies to you and promises you happiness, excitement, thrills, sexual fulfillment, and release. It even promises to medicate your pain. Why the promises? In addition to Satan's wanting to destroy you, porn is also about money, money, money. The porn industry is looking for customers, and they start young. They want customers for life.

One of the biggest lies of Internet pornography is, *Your number one need is sex.* It's not, but that's the line; your number one need is intimacy with God. Number two, if you've been blessed with a spouse, is the need for marital intimacy—a close emotional, physical, and spiritual connection with your wife.

"One of the first things porn, or any lust for that matter does when we engage in it, is disconnect us from our wives, or any true intimacy for that matter," writes Stuart Vogelman, in *Does Porn or a Husband's Wandering Eyes Hurt a Marriage?*[3] at marriagemissions.com.

The Adulteress Arrives

1. Respond to the statement: Viewing pornography is adultery. If you agree, why? If you do not agree, why not?
2. Compare a physical affair with viewing pornography? How are they alike? How are they different?
3. How would your wife respond to the assertion that viewing porn is adultery?

The Adulteress Affirms

1. How does Satan use pornography to flatter a Christian man?
2. How does pornography affect the sexual expectations a man has for his wife?
3. How does viewing pornography affect how a young man views women in general?

The Atmosphere

1. When would you most likely be tempted to view pornography? Describe specifically.
2. List what would get you thinking about pornography?
3. Give an example of the step-by-step rituals a man would go through to get to the point of viewing pornography.
4. What lies would Satan tell a Christian man to try to get him to look at pornography?
5. What are some ways a Christian man makes provision for the flesh (Romans 13:14)?
6. Practically, how would you clothe yourself with the presence of Jesus?

Always Available

1. In your opinion, at what age are we most vulnerable to pornography?
2. How has the availability of pornography, on the Internet, affected whether men in the church look at porn?

3. What do you think "Porn makes a man objectify a woman" means?
4. Give at least five practical steps a Christian man can take to avoid looking at pornography.

Anonymity Promised

1. Give at least five ways a man attempts to keep pornography viewing anonymous.
2. In your opinion, why does anyone think he can keep his porn viewing habit a secret?
3. How does the sin of viewing pornography cause you to do stupid things? Offer specific examples.

Absolutely Appealing to the Eye

1. What does Satan promise that porn will do for a man?
2. Why is pornography appealing to a man?
3. What is false about the statement, "Sex is your number one need"?

5: *C*ount the Cost

Then there is the aftermath that always occurs with pornography. As we continue our study of Proverbs 7 from last chapter, let's take a good look at what happens when pornography sinks its hook in. Again, related questions appear at the end of the chapter.

Aggressive

> *She is boisterous and rebellious,*
> *Her feet do not remain at home;*
> *So she seizes him and kisses him*
> *And with a brazen face she says to him:* (Proverbs 7:11, 13).

Pornography, like the adulteress, is aggressive. As we've noted, there was a time when a man had to look intentionally for pornography; now, pornography will find us!

Anyone who opens a porn site today will likely see three more sites that will hit the user. The onslaught aggressively comes at the mind so fast as to make a man become numb. A person ends up looking at something and is unsure how he even ended up there.

Pornography encourages us to act out in multiple ways, including masturbation, a subject we cover later in the book. Once that porn image infiltrates your mind, it lures you aggressively to "Come back!" It aggressively stalks your mind, inviting you to look again. That image pursues you with a passion. Pornography never satisfies; it leaves you with the insatiable desire to look again. Breaking free from it is extremely difficult, but with the power of our resurrected Jesus, it can be done.

Action Demanded

Suddenly he follows her
As an ox goes to the slaughter,
Or as one in fetters to the discipline of a fool (Proverbs 7:22).

Again, Satan has many traps that appeal to men, but none so devious as Internet pornography. The young man said yes to the prostitute. With Internet pornography, you are walking right into Satan's trap. It may seem sudden once you click on an Internet porn site, but this has been working in you for a long time. That action involved a lot of things that led up to the moment you clicked the mouse. What seems like a sudden decision can be traced back to days, months, and even years of compromise (and Satan knows it). The temptation quickly moves from your thought life into your actions.

There are many choices that take a toll on your ability to ward off temptation:

❑ A little compromise followed by a little more compromise.
❑ Not taking time to be holy.
❑ Not guarding your eyes.
❑ Not committing to daily spiritual disciplines.
❑ Not staying in love with Jesus Christ.
❑ Not paying attention to your wife.
❑ Not safeguarding the protective wall of holiness that should be strong in your life.

It all takes a toll. Like Samson, who lost his strength and didn't even know it. When the critical moment came, his strength failed because of compromise.

Amnesia Created

As an ox goes to the slaughter…
Until an arrow pierces through his liver;
As a bird hastens to the snare,
So he does not know that it will cost him his life (Proverbs 7:22–23).

Viewing pornography makes you forget everything that is important. That is a fact. In that moment of getting in the zone to look at porn, you do things that you never thought you would do. And when you finish, you wonder, *How could I have done that?*

✓ You forget your relationship with God.
✓ You forget your wife.
✓ You forget your children.
✓ You forget your position.
✓ You forget everything else.

Then, once you act out, your memory begins to come back.

Dr. Mark Kastleman, in his powerful book *The Drug of the New Millennium,* compares sexual arousal to a funnel. The wide part at the top represents normalcy. God wired the male brain so that when he is sexually aroused in a healthy marriage, he gives his full focus to his wife. During the courtship, the couple gets closer together. The act of physical love is the narrowest point of the funnel. Once that is completed, a healthy married couple will feel closer together than before.

Kastleman then compares healthy sex with pornography. The porn funnel is also wide at the top and narrow in the middle, but it is wide at the bottom. From the normal state at the top of the funnel, something triggers a man to think about watching porn. If that thought is not interrupted, the man will continue to focus on that, blocking out anything or anyone else.

Nothing exists but that pornographic image. God is forgotten, along with the man's commitment to Him, his wife, his children, the Bible, his job, and his relationships. Everything else is placed on the back burner. Pornography eradicates any categories such as pastors and nonpastors, husbands and singles, educated and uneducated, and rich and poor. The only remaining commonality is being male. (This narrowing process actually begins long before a Christian man is sitting in front of his computer looking at pornography. It is essential to form a spiritual strategy before the man is riveted to an image.)

The narrowest point at the center now represents a specific event—in this case, masturbation after having looked at pornography. After he has acted out sexually, the funnel actually begins to widen again. The man is left without support—physically, mentally, or emotionally. The resulting shame and guilt often leave him feeling more isolated, and the Christian man wonders, *How could I have done this?*

Annihilation Ensues

> *For many are the victims she has cast down,*
> *And numerous are all her slain.*
> *Her house is the way to Sheol,*
> *Descending to the chambers of death* (Proverbs 7:26–27).

Sexual sin is destructive. Its victims throughout history are too numerous to count. Does that mean sexual sin is worse than other sins in God's eyes? No. But the consequences of sexual sin are much worse and more hurtful to innocent people. The sins of Samson and David caused many to die.

Pornography has the touch of death. Just the stress alone of living a double life kills you emotionally and relationally.

✓ Porn kills marriages.
✓ Porn kills your relationship with your children.
✓ Porn kills creativity.
✓ Porn kills intimacy with God and your wife.
✓ Porn kills your witness.
✓ Porn kills your praise to God.
✓ Porn kills love.
✓ Porn kills time.
✓ Porn kills women's dignity and respect.
✓ Porn kills the innocence of children who see it.
✓ Porn kills the blessings of God.
✓ Porn kills your future.

Pornography necessitates that every Christian join the offensive.

Men, the good news is that the battle with pornography can be addressed, and you can win! You can move out of shame and into freedom! But you must be proactive and go on the offensive. You have to get aggressive. You can't just react. You have to attack. In fact, you can't wait to attack; you have to start right now.

It won't be easy, and it's not a quick-fix, one-time-will-do-it thing. It is a daily battle and a lifelong process. The fight, however, is worth the price to experience God's grace. Satan will lie and tell you that you cannot break free. Choose to believe God.

QUESTIONS CORRESPONDING TO:

Aggressive

1. How does pornography pursue you once you have seen it?
2. How is masturbation associated with pornography?
3. Why is masturbation a problem? Is it a sin? Why or why not?

Action Demanded

1. Give your opinion on how even the small compromises in your life can lead to looking at pornography.
2. How does failing to practice the spiritual disciplines contribute to your being open to viewing pornography?
3. How does temptation move from sinful thoughts to sinful actions?

Amnesia Created

1. What is there about pornography that makes you forget about what is most important in your life?
2. How does pornography hijack your brain?
3. How do you feel after you have looked at porn and sexually acted out?

Annihilation Ensues

1. How does porn kill:
   Spiritually?
   Emotionally?
   Relationally?
   Physically?
   Mentally?
2. Although in God's eyes all sin is sin, why do you think sexual sin seems to have greater consequences?

Say to wisdom,
"You are my sister."

—PROVERBS 7:4 —

Part 2

Use Our Battle Plan

6: S.H.I.E.L.D. Yourself

My son, keep my words
And treasure my commandments within you.
Keep my commandments and live,
And my teaching as the apple of your eye.
Bind them on your fingers;
Write them on the tablet of your heart.
Say to wisdom, "You are my sister."

—Proverbs 7:1–4

Notice the word *wisdom* (Proverbs 7:4). For our purposes, I'll define wisdom as the ability to follow the best course of action. It is a strategy, knowing how you are going to address the issue before the temptation comes. We will use the acrostic S-H-I-E-L-D to show you how to take the offensive.

Schedule Biblical Disciplines

Many Christian men are living without the practical power to overcome the thoughts to look at pornography. When the moment of temptation comes, they are in a spiritually weakened position. When you exercise spiritual disciplines, you can have that power. These disciplines should be practiced by every Christian man as he submits to the control and filling of the Holy Spirit.

❏ *Reading the Bible*—Immerse yourself into God's Word daily. I encourage you to get a one-year Bible and let God speak to you daily through it. You can read the Bible through in a year by committing about 12 minutes a day. You should also meditate on specific Scriptures that relate to your struggles. Find verses like 1 Corinthians 10:13 that encourage you with promises of God's help. *The Amplified Bible* puts it this way:

> *For no temptation (no trial regarded as enticing to sin),* [no matter how it comes or where it leads] *has overtaken you* and *laid hold on you that is not common to man* [that is, no temptation or trial has come to you that is beyond human resistance and that is not adjusted and adapted and belonging to human experience, and such as man can bear]. *But God is faithful [to His Word and to His compassionate nature], and He [can be trusted] not to let you be tempted* and *tried* and *assayed beyond your ability* and *strength of resistance* and *power to endure, but with the temptation He will* [always] *also provide the way out (the means of escape to* [c]*a landing place), that you may be capable* and *strong* and *powerful to bear up under it patiently.*

I contend that no Christian man should ever lay his head down on his pillow at night without having opened God's Word at some point during the day.

❑ *Praying*—Conversing with God daily helps you stay in His will. You can also pray for help with specific temptations as they arise, like Jesus did in the garden. In fact, 1 Thessalonians 5:17 encourages us to pray without ceasing. You can't pray too much.

❑ *Fasting*—Depriving yourself of food, as well as other wants, for a specific period of time helps you seek God more intensely. Fasting gives you a new dimension of spiritual power and perspective. However, make sure you research the topic in a book like *God's Chosen Fast,* and consult with a physician. Fasting the wrong way can be dangerous.

❑ *Committing to a Church*—Follow the example of the early Christians who met together regularly in Acts 2:42. Love, power, wisdom, and support are all available from your brothers and sisters in Christ.

If you don't exercise spiritual disciplines, God is not going to *zap* you! Something worse happens. In the moment of temptation, like Samson, you won't realize the power built from exercising these spiritual disciplines habitually. Spiritual disciplines will help you immensely in that moment you think about looking at pornography.

Have Godly Passion Greater Than Temptation

When it comes to your commitment to God, your passion must exceed the temptation you face. You can try all the methods and strategies to overcome the temptation to look at pornography, and they do help, but when it comes right down to it, it's a matter of how real your passion for God is. Your love for Jesus Christ—your desire to follow Him—has to become the passion of your life.

There is a prevalence of male enhancement ads, and men actually fall for them. Our concern needs to be enhancing our relationship with Jesus!

In his book, *The Obedience Option,* David Hegg illustrates what he calls "overwhelming faith." Hegg was talking to a young man who claimed that he couldn't stop his pattern of sleeping with different women. The young man knew it was wrong, but he also claimed that his sexual lust was inevitable. Therefore, it wasn't his fault, especially since God had created him with such strong desires.

Finally, Hegg interrupted the young man and said, "Suppose that I came into your room and caught you and your girlfriend as you were just starting this 'inevitable' process. Suppose I took out ten one-hundred-dollar bills and told you that they were yours if you [stopped]. What would you do?"

When the young man quickly said that he'd rather have the cash, Hegg asked, "So what happened to the irresistible force of lust?"

Then Hegg concluded:

> We both realized a very simple truth: one passion may seem irresistible until a greater passion comes along. . . . If we take this principle into the arena of righteous living, it comes out like this: the only way to overcome a passion for sin is with an overwhelming passion for righteousness.

Men, that greater passion in your life must be Jesus Christ! You will never stop looking at porn until you want Him more.

Invite Accountability

Guys, you will not win this battle alone, and you won't be the exception to that. You must have other godly men in your life who strive for purity. Find at least three men you can be accountable to. Put accountability software on all of your computers.

Don't trust yourself! Get other men who will ask you the hard questions about your purity. You can make it, if you invite accountability. Without it, you are a disaster waiting to happen. These are not comfortable conversations, so be ready to move out of your comfort zone and become transparent.

Eliminate Pornography Opportunities

Get rid of anything that contains pornography. As much as possible, eliminate the portals for porn. You don't have to be a hermit; however, eliminate everything and anything related to porn. It may even mean destroying your present computer.

Eliminate your premium cable channels. When you check into a hotel, have them turn off the adult channels. If your route to work is a problem, find a new one, even if it's longer. If you have "friends" who have porn, tell them it's a problem for you. If they can't respect that, then you need to change friends. It's that important.

List the Consequences

Rehearse the consequences. Go back and look at chapter 2 and see which ones apply to you. I want you to think about what it's going to cost you if you continue to view porn. Think about what it is doing to you spiritually. It is separating you from God—from His power, His peace, His joy. You have effectively blocked that from your life.

Each time a man views pornography, he impedes the ability of the Holy Spirit to direct him toward sanctification, and he slips further into depravity (1 Thessalonians 5:19). The more a man views pornography, the less likely he is to seek out God and live a pure life.

And don't forget about what it's going to do to your wife when she finds out, and she will find out. Think about looking into her heartbroken eyes as she realizes that she is not enough, that she can never measure up, that you cheated on her and betrayed her, and that she can never trust you again.

Even worse, you are putting out a welcome mat for Satan and his demons, opening a portal that allows them into your life.

Men, I am going to give you an illustrative template of a letter written to your wife. This is what you'll have to tell her *if* you continue to view porn, because, again, it is only a matter of time until she finds out.

Dear _____ (wife's name):

This letter I am reading to you serves as a confession to you that I have been viewing Internet pornography. Your husband has been unfaithful with his eyes. I took my eyes off of Jesus and put them on women on a Web site.

If I had put Jesus first, this would not have happened. If I had been thinking about how deeply it would hurt you, this would not have happened; however, I was thinking only of myself. I realize now that it has made you, my wife, feel that you do not measure up to these other women and will never be able to. I know that you understand that I will never be able to erase those images from my mind. I know that you will always wonder when we are having sex if I am thinking of you or them.

I realize that you might see this as adultery—that I have cheated on you—and you are right. According to what Jesus said, I have committed adultery against you in my heart. I have destroyed your trust in me. I have pierced your heart, causing you sorrow, anger, and insecurity. I have now put doubt in your mind, making you wonder if I have been faithful in other areas as well. I have even made you wonder if I might have had a real-life affair.

Now you understand why I asked you to do certain things sexually. It's because I wanted to act out what I saw on a porn site. Now you know why our intimate times together seemed more like sex acts than true intimacy.

You will now always wonder if I am looking at porn again. You will have doubts about what I am doing when I am traveling, when I am at work, and when you are away.

I have made you wonder what will happen if the kids find out, or if they already know. You will wonder if our son has accidentally stumbled onto something I downloaded or forgot to delete on the computer, forever altering his world of innocence. I have been responsible for a lifelong struggle for my son. You will also wonder how I could have looked at these sites, knowing that those women were someone's daughter.

Now you know why I neglected your needs. I was too busy focusing on my lust. I chose to put porn ahead of God, ahead of you, and ahead of our children. I have not respected you nor thought about what my viewing of porn will do to you and us. I wish a thousand times that I could get a redo on this. I wish I had never clicked that mouse. Things will never be the same.

Your Husband,

_____ (sign your name)

Now how many of you want to put your wife's name at the top and then sign *this* letter? *No man wants that!*

Discipline Your Eyes and Mind

Men, you must train your eyes and minds daily. Whatever your eyes see will affect your thought life.

You have to train them where to look and where not to look. You have to train them to look away immediately when there is something or someone that will take you There. You will find it is much simpler and easier to train your eyes when you keep your spiritual disciplines.

Some of you men have been Christians long enough to have advanced out of basic training in this area, but perhaps we need to revisit it. Your eyes will turn where you choose to turn them. Now, granted, there are those times when that cleavage is staring at you and you can't help that first look. However, it's what you do next that determines your purity.

Concerning your mind, guilt helps us do a pretty good job of confessing sinful thoughts. But replacing the thoughts is what we need to work on, and you replace them with Scripture. That's why I am encouraging you to train your mind for the next 31 days by meditating on specific Scriptures.

Men, if you have viewed pornography, you can be forgiven. God's grace will cover that sin, too! So the past is covered by the blood of Jesus, once you confess and repent. But from this moment on, you can be free. It will be a day-by-day—sometimes hour-by-hour—battle. Get the past settled now, and then take up this S.H.I.E.L.D.

1. What plan would you implement to include spiritual disciplines in your life? What would prevent you from acting on that plan?
2. How do spiritual disciplines give you strength to resist the lure to look at pornography?
3. How can you develop a greater passion for God?
4. Why is accountability with other godly men so vital?
5. Whom would you call at 2:00 A.M. if you were tempted? List at least seven men with whom you potentially could be accountable to on a regular basis.
6. What are the potential portals for pornography in your life, and how can you prevent temptation from entering them?
7. Read the letter of confession to the wife of a husband who has given into the temptation to view pornography. Respond to this question: What can you do now to keep from ever having to read this letter to *your* wife?
8. How can you discipline your eyes to keep from looking at porn or lusting after a woman?

7: *A*rm *Yourself*

There is nothing easy about overcoming a struggle with pornography. The battle is brutal, but winnable—in Christ. Breaking free is painful, but the rewards are far greater than the momentary rush of an image.

Please understand this clearly: the following 26 principles are not meant to replace therapy, workshops, or conferences that address issues of pornography or sexual addiction. But they are powerful weapons and tools you can use to turn the tide. Start taking charge of your life through the Bible, instead of letting pornography take you down its dark path. Each of these principles is based on Scripture. God's Word is our final authority.

Besides applying them to yourself, you can share these with other men who are struggling. Find a few who will go through this plan with you. You can strengthen and encouragement each other when you are in the trenches, holding each other accountable. You can also obtain a pocketsize copy to carry with you, which includes a daily prayer for each principle.

*A*dmit the Struggle

> *He who conceals his transgressions will not prosper, but he who confesses and forsakes them will find compassion* (Proverbs 28:13).

Admit, "Yes, pornography is a struggle for me." Rather than justifying or excusing it, simply admit your struggle to God, to yourself, and to caring people. There is great freedom in transparent acknowledgment. A secret possesses power—and Satan knows this. Shining the light of God's truth on anything sinful and hidden gives you the opportunity to break free. Once exposed, the chains of pornography begin to fall away and lose their power.

The first of the 12 steps of Sexaholics Anonymous gives a good reminder for you as you begin to pray:

> We admitted that we were powerless over lust—that our lives had become unmanageable.

> You can never conquer sin with an excuse.
> —Author Unknown

*B*reak Free

This is going to be one of the hardest battles you have ever fought, but you must believe it is winnable.

> For the weapons of our warfare are not of the flesh, but divinely powerful for the destruction of fortresses. We are destroying speculations and every lofty thing raised up against the knowledge of God, and we are taking every thought captive to the obedience of Christ (2 Corinthians 10:4–5).

Battling pornography involves spiritual warfare. Your flesh (your sinful nature) is going to fight back. Your mind is going to threaten you, trying to convince you that you can't survive without looking at pornography. Satan is going to bring tempting opportunities like never before. But you can break free! That is truth.

You can experience God's overcoming and healing power. "There is always a choice when it comes to breaking free from addictive behaviors," says Dr. Randy Hyde. God is greater than your stronghold!

*C*ome Clean with God

Confess viewing pornography as sin. "If we confess our sins, He is faithful and righteous to forgive us our sins and to cleanse us from all unrighteousness" (1 John 1:9). But true confession also involves repentance. Repentance breaks the cycle of sin. Repentance involves brokenness. It is a moment in time when God, through His Holy Spirit, convicts you to truly change the direction you are going. You recognize your sin as being destructive in your life and contrary to

God's will. You experience an overwhelming sense of sorrow for what you have done. You vow in God's power to no longer do that which God has revealed as sin in your life. Where there is no change, there has been no repentance.

The process of repentance involves:

1. Recognition—You have an acute awareness that you have sinned.
2. Responsibility—You blame no one else for your choices and actions.
3. Release—You confess your specific sin(s) to God.
4. Request—You ask God to forgive you.
5. Remove—You distance yourself from that which causes you to fall into sin.
6. Return—You once again strive to do only the will of God.
7. Rejoice—You *can* know victory and freedom from sin and guilt. By faith, claim God's forgiveness.

*D*estroy All Porn Stashes Now

> *Therefore, putting aside all filthiness and all that remains of wickedness, in humility receive the word implanted, which is able to save your souls* (James 1:21).

Everywhere that you have pornography—on your personal computer, cell phone, or office computer—destroy it now! If you possess any pornographic books, magazines, DVDs, or recordings on your TiVo or DVR—destroy them now! Get violent in your destruction of your secret stashes of pornography. You may even need to destroy your present computer. The cost of not destroying a computer with porn on it is much greater than the cost of destroying it. I promise you that if you have children, they will find your pornography, and it will adversely affect their lives.

Many men who battle with viewing pornography began their struggle by finding their dad's stash. You do not want to be responsible for causing your son or daughter to stumble spiritually because of your sin.

*E*liminate Pornography Portals, Outlets, and Access Anywhere

"But put on the Lord Jesus Christ, and make no provision for the flesh in regard to its lusts" (Romans 13:14). Think of any places in your life where pornography has an outlet and eliminate it. Here are some ideas:

- Cancel premium cable on your home television.
- When going to a hotel, ask the front desk to disable the adult movie channels.
- Stop renting or going to movies with sexual content.
- Disable your webcam.
- Cancel your membership to any pornographic sites.
- Refuse to open unsolicited emails.
- Stop deliberately driving by billboards or businesses that encourage sinful sexual thoughts.
- Immediately throw away catalog advertisements that feature scantily dressed women.
- Refuse to read books or magazines that could encourage lustful thoughts.
- Cease channel surfing for sexually explicit material. Try putting the remote control in an out-of-the way place after a certain time at night.
- Tell the woman in your life that seeing scantily dressed women on television is a problem for you, and ask for her help.
- Have a family meeting and share that your home is and always will be a pornography-free home. Address the dangers of pornography with your family. That gives you an additional layer of accountability.
- Insist on Internet accountability software on your work computer.

*F*reedom in God's Truth

Embrace it now! "And you will know the truth, and the truth will make you free" (John 8:32). Jesus said that only the truth will make you free. You must believe that acting on God's truth, and continuing to act on that truth, will bring freedom to your life. The truth is: viewing pornography is sin. The truth is, when you act on God's Word, He will give you the power to break free from the chains of pornography.

*G*uard Your Heart

Intentionally protect your thoughts and feelings.

> *Above all else, guard your heart, for everything you do flows from it* (Proverbs 4:23 NIV).

I made a covenant with my eyes not to look lustfully at a young woman (Job 31:1 NIV).

Do not sharply rebuke an older man, but rather appeal to him as a father, to the younger men as brothers, the older women as mothers, and the younger women as sisters, in all purity (1 Timothy 5:1–2).

You guard your heart by guarding your eyes. You train your eyes by immediately looking away from people and images that create lust. Unguarded eyes, unguarded thoughts, and unguarded feelings eventually lead to sinful actions.

Viewing porn promotes "pornifying" women, that is, seeing women as sexual objects. Since the porn you viewed is stored in your mind, Satan will attempt to rewind and play, to encourage you to see women as objects for sex. Pornography changes your perspective of women from lovingly created companions to objects of lust.

When you see another woman, look in her eyes, look in her eyes, look in her eyes! Don't "check her out." Despite your best efforts, you still might slip up. If you do, guard yourself by confessing your sin immediately and placing it under Christ's authority.

*H*onesty

If you are serious about breaking free from pornography, total honesty with your spouse is essential. "Do not lie to one another, since you laid aside the old self with its evil practices" (Colossians 3:9). Be honest with your wife. This will be extremely painful for her, so bathe this in much prayer. Your transparency with your wife about your struggle with pornography demonstrates your seriousness about committing to purity, to God, and to her. Trust has been broken, and this is the first painful step toward regaining that trust.

One suggestion for communicating your struggle with your wife is to write your thoughts down in a letter. Read it to her so she can see you are committed to doing the right thing. She will probably feel an array of emotions — anger, betrayal, hurt. The impact that your choice has made on her must be a constant reminder to you that this pain was unnecessary. This builds another wall of protection that reminds you never to go back again.

*I*nstall Internet Filtering

This safeguard will block sexually inappropriate material on all your computers. Additionally, accountability software will report any sites you visit that are sexually inappropriate.

> *For this is the will of God, your sanctification; that is, that you abstain from sexual immorality; that each of you know how to possess his own vessel in sanctification and honor, not in lustful passion, like the Gentiles who do not know God* (1 Thessalonians 4:3–5).

You need both accountability and filtering tools on every computer. The accountability software reports your Internet activity to a person you choose. While this adds a layer of accountability, it does not block pornography or questionable sites. That is why you also need filtering software that can block sexually inappropriate sites and emails.

Although this software is vital, it will not offer 100 percent certainty that all pornography will be blocked. These are external tools that help protect the heart, not make it pure. At the heart of the matter is that you do the right thing. Covenant Eyes (Covenanteyes.com has some of the best software programs available.

*J*oin a Support Group

A support group will specifically address the issue you are struggling with. Begin with a group at your local church. If your church does not have a group, find one that is closest to you.

> *Blessed be the God and Father of our Lord Jesus Christ, the Father of mercies and God of all comfort, who comforts us in all our affliction so that we will be able to comfort those who are in any affliction with the comfort with which we ourselves are comforted by God* (2 Corinthians 1:3–4).

> *Therefore, confess your sins to one another, and pray for one another so that you may be healed. The effective prayer of a righteous man can accomplish much* (James 5:16).

There are effective 12-step groups available as well. (Contact local churches for information.) Two of the most popular Christian ones are Celebrate Recovery (celebraterecovery.com) and L.I.F.E. Ministries International (freedomeveryday.org).

No one gets completely well without help. See the resources at the back of this book, and consult with your pastor or other Christian leader who can help you enlist support.

*K*eep Resources Available

"The beginning of wisdom is: Acquire wisdom; and with all your acquiring, get understanding" (Proverbs 4:7). Besides hanging onto this book, look into the other resources in this book. They are highly recommended and will help you in your struggle. Ask others at support groups what has helped them. Build a library to arm yourself for this lifetime battle.

*L*ist the People Most Important to You

Ask yourself, *Is porn more important than they are?* and *How is my viewing of porn affecting each of them?* "But seek first His kingdom and His righteousness, and all these things will be added to you" (Matthew 6:33). If you continue to view pornography, you are putting in jeopardy everyone who matters most to you in life.

You cannot love your wife and children the way God intended if you are viewing porn. Think about the question, "How would their knowledge of what I have done affect our relationship?"

Pornography is exclusive; it demands first place! God demands first place. The two cannot live together in harmony. Choose God.

*M*asturbation

It is a sinful sexual activity when accompanied by porn or lust. "You say, 'I am allowed to do anything'—but not everything is good for you. And even though 'I am allowed to do anything,' I must not become a slave to anything" (1 Corinthians 6:12 NLT).

> *You know the next commandment pretty well, too: "Don't go to bed with another's spouse." But don't think you've preserved your virtue*

simply by staying out of bed. Your heart can be corrupted by lust even quicker than your body. Those leering looks you think nobody notices—they also corrupt. Let's not pretend this is easier than it really is. If you want to live a morally pure life, here's what you have to do: You have to blind your right eye the moment you catch it in a lustful leer. You have to choose to live one-eyed or else be dumped on a moral trash pile (Matthew 5:27–29 *The Message*).

It is not possible to masturbate without sin if do so with an image of pornography in your mind or while you are viewing porn. This is highly enslaving and self-centered. God never intended for sex to be a solo act. Masturbating while viewing a pornographic image creates a sinful imprint on your mind.

Masturbation can become a prison for a Christian man, a prison he freely walks into but forever struggles to escape. Pornography viewing keeps you going back into the prison and, as C. S. Lewis said, "The danger is that of coming to love the prison."

Name and Cell Numbers

Have this information readily available for at least three men you can call at any time and be accountable to consistently.

> *Two are better than one because they have a good return for their labor. For if either of them falls, the one will lift up his companion. But woe to the one who falls when there is not another to lift him up. Furthermore, if two lie down together they keep warm, but how can one be warm alone? And if one can overpower him who is alone, two can resist him. A cord of three strands is not quickly torn apart* (Ecclesiastes 4:9–12).

Call one of those men when you are tempted to begin the rituals you go through that lead to viewing pornography, or when you are being triggered by something or someone that would tempt you to act.

> *An unaccountable man is an accident waiting to happen* (XXXChurch .com).

Here is a list of questions that one of your helpmates should be asking you when you call. You can also find variations of these questions in numerous Web sites and publications.

1. Have you been in a situation with a woman anywhere this past week that others might deem compromising?
2. Have you exposed yourself to any sexually explicit material?
3. Have you spent adequate time in Bible study and prayer?
4. Have you given top priority to your family?
5. Have you just lied to me about any of the previous four questions?

*O*wn Your Struggle

Take responsibility! Change begins when you take responsibility and own your pornography struggle as your own problem. Stop blaming anyone or anything else. "Yes, each of us will give a personal account to God" (Romans 14:12 NLT).

You chose to look at porn; nobody made you. Stop pointing the finger at your past hurts, unfulfilled emotions, the way you were raised, or what your wife is doing or not doing as the reasons you look at pornography.

*P*lan for a Porn-Free Environment

> *All of you must keep awake (give strict attention, be cautious and active) and watch and pray, that you may not come into temptation. The spirit indeed is willing, but the flesh is weak* (Matthew 26:41 AMP).

Visually surround yourself with what really matters most to you. For your computer, activate a screensaver with pictures of the most important people in your life. Or install one with Scriptures. Place sticky notes with Scriptures on your computer.

Share your computer password with your wife or godly friend. Place your computer in an open place where anyone can see.

Revisit the Eliminate section above. Cancel the premium channels on your cable. That can be a huge temptation. You may need to take a different route to work or stop going near places where you encounter sexually oriented material or obvious temptations.

*Q*uit Thinking Porn Isn't Damaging

Don't deceive yourself into believing that porn isn't negatively affecting your relationships. It is!

> *Flee immorality. Every other sin that a man commits is outside the body, but the immoral man sins against his own body. Or do you not know that your body is a temple of the Holy Spirit who is in you, whom you have from God, and that you are not your own? For you have been bought with a price: therefore glorify God in your body* (1 Corinthians 6:18–20).

You cannot view porn and be the . . .

Christian
husband
father
son
brother
church member
friend . . .

that God has called you to be! Pornography is death to relationships. It never has a neutral effect on a man, especially a Christian man. Pornography negatively impacts every areas of a Christian's life.

*R*ituals

A ritual begins when you start thinking about looking at pornography. What rituals do you go through to look at it?

> *No temptation has overtaken you but such as is common to man; and God is faithful, who will not allow you to be tempted beyond what you are able, but with the temptation will provide the way of escape also, so that you will be able to endure it* (1 Corinthians 10:13).

> A ritual is a process or procedure you go through to do what you do, in this case sexually acting out. It is what you do to get ready for

sexually acting out. When the ritual begins, the battle is lost.

—Mark Laaser, Faithful and True Ministries

Begin with your actual viewing of pornography and work backwards. Trace your steps. Before you looked at porn, recall each step you took to get there. The more specific you are, the more chance you have to break free. Ask yourself:

What did I think about?

Was I replaying a past image? Was I thinking about someone other than my wife? Was I thinking about a certain feeling I usually feel when I look at pornography?

Where was I?

Was I at work, home, in a hotel room, on a business trip? Was it a place in the mall, the grocery store, or a restaurant? Where am I more likely to think about looking at pornography?

When was it?

What time of day was it when I last viewed pornography? Is there a consistent pattern?

Who was near?

Was my wife at home? Was it at night when everyone was asleep, or during the day at work? What circumstances made it easier for me to reach the point of viewing porn?

Once you determine the answers to these questions, you can deliberately address them and place "exit signs" over them.

An exit sign shows the way out in case of a fire. Lust is like a fire. Because you are a follower of Jesus, God has promised an exit. But you have to know where it is, and you can't wait until the fire burns down the building—or in this case, burns you.

Build an exit by rehearsing what you will do when next confronted with the temptation to look at pornography. Your specific escape route needs to be mapped out in advance.

For example, if you know that when your wife goes to bed early, you take the opportunity to look at porn, realize this tendency and create a way out. Force yourself to go to bed early with her, or put filters to block online activity past a certain time. Know your way out. If you are single or your wife is going to be out of town, ask one of your accountability relationships to call you at the specific time you would more likely be tempted to look at pornography. The important point is that you must do this *prior* to the temptation. Waiting until the moment of temptation usually means the battle will be lost.

Stop the Rituals

> Now therefore, my sons, listen to me, and pay attention to the words of my mouth. Do not let your heart turn aside to her ways, do not stray into her paths (Proverbs 7:24–25).

You can stop the rituals by interrupting them, by taking a different course of action. Be aware of the steps you take prior to viewing porn. Take specific action to change those steps.

For example, if you've identified certain times you are most vulnerable to looking at porn, find something specific you can do then (exercising, calling a loved one or friend, developing a hobby). You are familiar with the usual feelings, places, people, thoughts, and atmosphere. The key is interrupting the pattern you follow when you look at pornography.

Travel without your laptop and use the computer in the business center of the hotel. A commitment to radical purity motivates you to stop the thinking that leads to viewing pornography.

Triggers

A trigger is a stimulus that places you in an atmosphere encouraging you to view pornography, and even to act out sexually. Something in your brain reacts to an idea, a thought, a possibility. If you know what triggers your temptation, take decisive action to address it before it occurs.

> Therefore, since we have so great a cloud of witnesses surrounding us, let us also lay aside every encumbrance and the sin which so

easily entangles us, and let us run with endurance the race that is set before us (Hebrews 12:1).

A trigger can easily take place when you are Hungry, Angry, Lonely, and Tired.

—HALT" (Sexaholics Anonymous).

Triggers are vulnerable areas in your life that promote looking at pornography. To identify what triggers you to view porn, think about the last three times you looked at it, and then ask the following questions:

Was there a certain visual image?

Was it a lingerie catalog? Was there a certain billboard or sign that made me think about pornography? Was it a certain woman at work or at the gym?

Are there certain places?

Is it easier to think about looking at pornography at a friend's house? Or at a restaurant, or away from home in a certain town?

Is there a certain feeling?

Is there an emotional state that leads to higher vulnerability? Are things worse when I am emotionally spent, depressed, stressed out, tense from a relationship, responsible for everything and everyone, sexually frustrated, bored, in pain, angry, unappreciated, or feeling like a failure?

Are there certain words?

Am I affected by what people say? Or do certain types of music make it harder to say No? Do certain television shows trigger it?

Mark Laaser says, in *Taking Every Thought Captive*, "Basically, a trigger is anything that goes from your five senses to your brain. You hear them, see them, smell them, taste them, or physically feel them."

*U*ncover Untrue Beliefs

You are of your father the devil, and you want to do the desires of your father. He was a murderer from the beginning, and does not

stand in the truth because there is no truth in him. Whenever he
speaks a lie, he speaks from his own nature, for he is a liar and the
father of lies (John 8:44).

We often find ourselves believing certain common ideas which, when examined more closely, turn out to be untrue. Some of these may include:

1. If people knew the real me, they would not accept me; they would reject me.
2. I'm not sure that even God loves me anymore.
3. I can't survive without looking at porn.
4. Sex is my number one need.
5. No other Christian man is having this kind of struggle with porn.

Each one of these is a lie. The truth is, you are loved for who you are, and you are not alone. God unconditionally loves you. Nothing you could ever do would make Him not love you, but He loves you too much to let you to suffer in your lust-filled condition. Your greatest need is not for pornography or sex, but for healthy relationships and intimacy with God.

Visualize the Consequences

But each one is tempted when he is carried away and enticed by
his own lust. Then when lust has conceived, it gives birth to sin; and
when sin is accomplished, it brings forth death. Do not be deceived,
my beloved brethren (James 1:14–16).

Men seem to be wired in such a way that pornography hijacks the proper functioning of their brains and has a long-lasting effect on their thoughts and lives. Pornography is "visually magnetic" to the male brain. . . . Enough is never enough.

—William Struthers, *Wired for Intimacy*

Pornography has an escalating effect and will take you further and deeper. That is the nature of porn. Think about the potential consequences to your marriage, your children, your job, your relationships, your walk with God, and your reputation. A few of those consequences are public humiliation; destroyed intimacy and trust with your wife; children who end up compromised spiritually, morally, and emotionally; a ruined reputation; financial difficulties; legal action; loss of the joy and power of salvation; and, worst of all, a growing distance between you and God.

> The turning point for most men is when they get caught either by their wives, their bosses, or by the police.
>
> —Meg Wilson, from *Hope After Betrayal*

*W*ar Against Sinful Thoughts

> *For the weapons of our warfare are not of the flesh, but divinely powerful for the destruction of fortresses. We are destroying speculations and every lofty thing raised up against the knowledge of God, and we are taking every thought captive to the obedience of Christ* (2 Corinthians 10:4–5).

This is where the war with porn will be won or lost. Utilize the "S.T.O.P. the Thought" method. Dr. Arch Hart suggests that when a sinful thought enters your mind, use the technique of saying out loud, "Stop the thought," to interrupt it. A method a colleague and I developed was applying the acrostic S.T.O.P. to your thought life in order to win the war against sinful thinking.

S—*Sinful thoughts are to be confessed immediately* (1 John 1:9).

T—*Think on these things.* Replace the sinful thought you just confessed with biblical truth (Philippians 4:8). An effective way to do this is through biblical meditation, taking a Scripture and reading it, reflecting upon it, praying it back to God, and then asking the Holy Spirit to speak through that Scripture.

O—*Order the thought to get under the authority of Jesus Christ.* Paul teaches us that immediately when a sinful thought enters our mind, by an act of the will, in the power of the Holy Spirit, you command the thought to leave your mind and place it under the blood of Jesus, in the name of Jesus. You order the thought, commanding it to leave. You cannot deal lightly or gently with a sinful thought.

P—*Pursue the mind of Christ* (Philippians 2:5).

You pursue the mind of Christ by:
• renewing your mind daily through Scripture,
• practicing thinking about God things, and
• disciplining your mind through the spiritual disciplines.
> —Jay Dennis and Marilyn Jeffcoat, *Taming Your Private Thoughts*

e**X**ercise Spiritual Disciplines

> *Discipline yourself for the purpose of godliness* (1 Timothy 4:7).

> Discipline, for the Christian, begins with the body. We have only one.
> It is this body that is the primary material given to us for sacrifice.
> We cannot give our hearts to God and keep our bodies for ourselves.
> —Elisabeth Elliot

Growing spiritually is vital to your overcoming the pornography war. With the exception of fasting, each of the disciplines should be practiced daily. Like building muscles, the more you practice these, the stronger you will become.
1. Bible reading
2. Prayer
3. Scripture memory
4. Fasting
5. Journaling
6. Worship
7. Meditation
8. Solitude (time alone with God to listen)

Yield to God
Give yourself to Him daily and confess that the only power you have over porn is the power given by His Holy Spirit as you surrender to Him.

And do not go on presenting the members of your body to sin as instruments of unrighteousness; but present yourselves to God as those alive from the dead, and your members as instruments of righteousness to God (Romans 6:13).

This principle cannot be overstated. As you surrender to the Holy Spirit, the practical power that comes from the resurrected Jesus allows you to say Yes to God's will and No to pornography. Being daily filled with the Holy Spirit gives you supernatural power to address the temptation to look at pornography.

Zero in on the Zones

Identify where you will be tempted to think about looking at pornography, then avoid those zones. "Do not be deceived: 'Bad company corrupts good morals'" (1 Corinthians 15:33).

❑ There are certain people who do not share your passion to live in purity. To be a godly man, you cannot spend all your time with ungodly people. They will maneuver you in the wrong direction. There may be someone you need to cut loose from your life.

❑ There are certain places you should never go, places you know you will be tempted. Certain places are tempting to every man, but there are also specific places that may have a unique temptation to you. Stay away from them. Don't go there!

❑ There are certain situations you should never allow yourself to get into, such as conversing intimately with another woman in a chat room or on Facebook. Don't allow yourself to get into those predicaments.

Specifically identify these zones and place them as off limits.

You must constantly put these 26 principles to work. If pornography has disrupted your life, home, work, marriage, or other relationships, I encourage you to act now. Don't wait one more minute. The longer you wait to deal with the issue of pornography in your life, the more enslaved you will become.

Let freedom in your life begin today!

8: *Disarm* Masturbation

> I vote no on masturbation. There may be other reasons why it is wrong. For now I rest my vote on the inevitable sexual images which accompany masturbation and which turn women into sexual objects. The sexual thoughts that enable masturbation do not help any man to treat women with greater respect. Therefore masturbation produces real and legitimate guilt and stands in the way of obedience.
>
> —John Piper, *Missions and Masturbation,* Desiring God.org

Pornography connects with a man's hidden habit, and we could not possibly consider this book complete without discussing that habit: *masturbation.* The subject has been taboo, awkward, and embarrassing to discuss in public, much less in church. Look at some of the bizarre misinformation out there.

It will:

• make you go blind,
• cause you to have hairy palms,
• cause cancer, or
• cause you to go insane.

These myths are laughable; however, others are more believable:

• Masturbation is something you do when you're young, but you will grow out of it.
• It is bad for your health.
• It doesn't happen after you get married.
• It is unnatural.
• Only certain kinds of people do it.

Cory Silverberg, in an About.com article, "Myths About Masturbation," humor-ously commented on the statement, "Only certain kinds of people do it":

> Survey research debunks this myth that only certain people masturbate. Whether you are 19 or 99, religious and conservative or secular and liberal, whether you are a parent, grandparent, uncle or aunt, whether you get around on your own two legs or use a wheelchair, scooter, crutches, or roller-skates to get around, almost everyone has masturbated at some point in their lives, and most of us continue to do so.[1]

Christian Men Masturbate

Statistical information varies on the subject. Some report:

• 85 to 95 percent of men masturbate at least once a month.

• 96 percent of Christian males under the age of 20 masturbate regularly.

• 61 percent of Christian married men masturbate regularly.[2]

• 16 percent of those married Christian men use pornography to stimulate themselves to masturbate.[3]

Based on years of pastoral counseling, I would suggest that the numbers are higher. Whatever the exact statistic, people who use porn almost always act out with masturbation. Sadly, masturbating while viewing pornography creates emptiness, shame, guilt, and lack of fulfillment. Intimacy, that soul and body connection with your mate, is missing.

What God Says

Although masturbation and pornography are closely linked, masturbation has its own separate issues. Let's examine some of them through the light of the Bible, because God always speaks through His Word as we genuinely seek after the truth. We must consider the principles of God's Word to reveal what kind of issue masturbation is for each one of us.

Masturbation Tied to Pornography

If your masturbation habit is linked to porn, then it is without-a-doubt sin-ful. There is simply no possibility of not sinning while viewing pornography and masturbating. With pornography comes masturbation. Sometimes it's the other way around; with masturbation, pornography can enter a man's life as he looks for something to further stimulate him. When that happens, it becomes sinful.

The reality is, masturbation feeds pornography and pornography feeds masturbation. Most often, where you find one, you will find the other. "Those addicted to porn are almost always addicted to masturbation."[4]

Masturbation Can Hinder Your Walk with God

Does masturbation draw you closer to God or cause you to feel distant from Him? Does it help you grow spiritually, or does it drag you down? You should not practice anything that hurts your relationship with the Lord by reducing your love, cooling your fire, causing you to feel distant, or taking your eyes off of Him.

The Apostle Paul reminds us,

> *The sinful nature wants to do evil, which is just the opposite of what the Spirit wants. And the Spirit gives us desires that are the opposite of what the sinful nature desires. These two forces are constantly fighting each other* (Galatians 5:17 NLT).

There is a constant pull by the world around you, by your flesh, and by Satan to bring you into a downward spiral spiritually. Paul's appeal to the Colossian Church could apply to our subject:

> *Therefore if you have been raised up with Christ, keep seeking the things above, where Christ is, seated at the right hand of God. Set your mind on the things above, not on the things that are on earth* (Colossians 3:1–2).

Addictive Masturbation

Paul made his own conviction clear to the Corinthian believers: "All things are lawful for me, but not all things are profitable. All things are lawful for me, but I will not be mastered by anything" (1 Corinthians 6:12). *The Message* puts the verse this way, "Just because something is technically legal doesn't mean that it's spiritually appropriate. If I went around doing whatever I thought I could get by with, I'd be a slave to my whims."

For many Christian men, masturbation has become an addictive activity that has enslaved them. Addictions control one's energy, time, thoughts, and plans. We end up looking for opportunities to feed our habit. Paul warns, "But put on the Lord Jesus Christ, and make no provision for the flesh in regard to its lusts" (Romans 13:14). We must not look for opportunities to lust; in fact, we must not even put ourselves in the position to encounter things that we know that might lead us to lust.

For you it may be the computer, the TV, magazines, places you go, the checkout stand at the grocery store, or mail ads that feature scantily dressed women. Men, don't even pick up those catalogs or magazines that trigger lust within you. Don't click on it either. Do everything possible (and then some) to remove yourself from them, thus removing the opportunity for them to work in your mind. Anything you are a slave to robs you of your freedom in Christ. In Christ, you are free *not* to do those things that will put you in chains.

William Struthers, in his book *Wired for Intimacy,* says, "Of all the forms of sexual acting out for men, masturbation is inherently the most isolating and potentially shaming." He further says, "With repeated sexual acting out in the absence of a partner, a man will be bound and attached to the image and not a person. The outcome is enslavement.

Mental Adultery in Masturbation

Jesus was clear that lusting after someone who is not your wife is committing adultery in your heart, or mental adultery. "You have heard that it was said, '*You shall not commit adultery*'; but I say to you that everyone who looks at a woman with lust for her has already committed adultery with her in his heart" (Matthew 5:27–28: emphasis mine).

If you are married, you need to ask yourself, *Can I masturbate and not visualize mental images of anyone but my wife?* Obviously, if there is pornography involved, you have already crossed the line into sin. The thought life is the battleground where Satan will look for any opportunity to defeat you. If your mind is wandering toward that woman you saw at work, the gym, online, on a billboard, at the game, or in that airbrushed picture, sin is at the door knocking enthusiastically. If you are a single adult, I don't think it is possible to masturbate without lust. If you can, you are a rare exception, since masturbation almost always involves fantasizing about someone of the opposite sex.

Masturbation Affects Your Marriage

Masturbation can affect intimacy with your wife—both emotionally and sexually. Self-sex can create a distance between you and your wife, rather than drawing you closer to her. The temptation with masturbation is to put your needs above your wife's needs, in direct opposition to Scripture found in 1 Corinthians 7:2–5.

One of my seminary professors at Fuller Theological Seminary, Dr. Archibald Hart, conducted a study on the sexual activity of men, which he published in his book, *The Sexual Man*. Regarding how masturbation affects a man's relationship to his wife, he points out:

> Such obsessions are not healthy for marriages. The husband eventually finds intercourse less satisfying. The use of fantasy transports him into the arms of someone else or into his favorite porn movie. He doesn't give his sexual relationship with his partner the priority and intimacy it deserves. There is no incentive to build a better sexual bond.
>
> I have treated many such marriages. The husband spends so much time secretly masturbating that he never has the energy or interest to romance his wife. Because she is not romanced she loses interest, and the relationship cools and dies. The secretiveness of his masturbating, in the meantime, feeds the taboo excitement that keeps him sexually isolated. Not a healthy cycle!

Hart goes on to say that there are three conditions under which masturbation is clearly wrong or destructive:
1. When it is used to avoid sexual intimacy or punish a partner by satisfying oneself.
2. When it is used to fulfill an addictive urge.
3. When it is used to foster lust or a desire for others.[5]

Will masturbation rob you of time you should be spending with your wife, meeting her needs emotionally, physically, or spiritually? Will it put the focus on you instead of on her? Whatever takes your time, energy and focus away from your wife and puts it on yourself is not consistent with the teachings of God's Word (see Ephesians 5:25–28).

Many men, even Christian men, view sexual relations with their wives as little more than an opportunity to masturbate. They are concerned only with pleasing themselves. They do not realize that God gave them their sexual organs, not just for their own pleasure, but also for the pleasure of their wives (1 Corinthians 7:4). They have never learned that in sexual relations, as in all other areas of life, "It is more blessed to give than to receive" (Acts 20:35).[6]

Pray About Masturbation

Have you brought this matter before the Lord and asked Him to show you what is right? God honors our sincere requests.

> This is the confidence which we have before Him, that if we ask anything according to His will, He hears us. And if we know that He hears us in whatever we ask, we know that we have the requests which we have asked from Him (1 John 5:14–15).

When you have a feeling of turmoil or conviction in your spirit telling you, *This is not the right thing to do,* talk to the Lord about it. He will shed light on the matter. When you pray, give God the freedom to answer—without any defensiveness or excuses on your part. You must be willing to do what God tells you, for God says, "And whatever you do or say, do it as a representative of the Lord Jesus, giving thanks through him to God the Father" (Colossians 3:17 NLT). Begin with, "God, I will obey whatever You tell me to do."

Masturbation Affects How You Look at Women

Does masturbating cause you to view women as sex objects? If it results in your looking at them in an impure way, then you have your answer. We know that pornography adversely affects the way men look at women. Viewing pornography is like putting on a "Lust Lens," seeing women through the eyes of lust. Masturbation could have that same affect.

In the Old Testament, Job understood this principle. He said, "I made a covenant with my eyes not to look with lust at a young woman" (Job 31:1 NLT). *The Message* says it this way, "I made a solemn pact with myself never to undress a girl with my eyes."

The Christian man should see another woman as his mother, if she is older; as his sister, if she is around the same age; or as his daughter, if she is younger. If masturbation causes you to violate this principle, it's time to give it up.

Masturbation Condemnation

You need to ask yourself what affect masturbating is having on your emotions. Are you riddled with guilt? Does it bring shame into your life? Are you embarrassed about it? Would you just die if someone else knew about your secret? If a weaker Christian brother found out, would it cause him to stumble?

> *Therefore let us not judge one another anymore, but rather determine this — not to put an obstacle or a stumbling block in a brother's way. It is good not to eat meat or to drink wine, or to do anything by which your brother stumbles* (Romans 14:13, 21).

Holy Spirit Conviction

The Holy Spirit, who makes His home in the body of the believer, will let you know when He is offended. That is called conviction, the sense that something is wrong that He wants to help you fix. This is different than feeling condemned, the sense that you are not worth the effort. Jesus told us that one of the roles of the Holy Spirit would be to convict us when we sin (John 16:8). If the Holy Spirit is convicting you, confess it to God immediately, turn away from it, ask God to forgive you, and through His strength daily depend on Him not to go there again.

There is victory over masturbation. It won't be easy, but you have all of God's resources at your disposal to fight and win this battle. If you have become enslaved by masturbation, apply these steps to disarm its power:

Confess Your Sin

Repent, and seek God's forgiveness. Masturbation is not beyond the mercy of God. He has never said, "Not that particular sin," to true repentance. Confess the viewing of pornography as sin. Confess lusting after someone not your wife as sin (Matthew 5:28).

True repentance means that you are broken. You grieve because you have offended your heavenly Father. Seek His forgiveness and declare that, in His power, you will not do that again. Repentance breaks sin's cycle. God has gone on record that He will forgive (1 John 1:9). Trust what He says, not how you feel.

Eradicate Pornography

Obviously, for you to overcome your masturbation habit, you must commit to living a pornography-free life, beginning right now. This is absolutely essential. If you are serious about purity and seeing God work, you cannot tolerate any pornography in your life. Period.

Sadly, the porn images stored in your memory become part of your struggle with lust and masturbation. Even though God gives us ways to address the sins of the past, there is no redo. However, beginning right now, you can eradicate pornography and masturbation from the present and future (Colossians 3:5).

Replace Porn With Scripture

Take the 31-Day challenge at Join1MillionMen.org by committing to not only confess sinful thoughts, but also to replace them with a specific Scripture. At the instant pornography makes its evil onslaught on your eyes, turn to God. Focus instead on 2 Corinthians 10:4–5 and Psalm 119:9 for starters. Your struggles with masturbation and pornography are won in your thought life.

Responding to a young Christian's struggle with masturbation, Randy Alcorn writes the following:

> The battle with masturbation is won or lost in the mind. The more we watch television, movies, etc., and certainly any kind of magazine or Internet pornography, the more addicted we'll become. Christ offers deliverance, but we must draw upon the empowerment of his grace for victory.
>
> God will gladly forgive someone for masturbating, but there needs to be genuine repentance, which involves taking radical steps to control influences on our minds—e.g., cutting off the Internet connection, staying away from certain places and people, only

seeing decent movies, turning off the TV (the commercials alone are a huge problem).

Again, the biggest key to overcoming masturbation is screening out all the ungodly input that tempts us toward it and fools us into thinking we need to have sex. Sex is a want, but not a need. There are many people with sexual natures called to lifelong singleness. Abstinence is not impossible. (Even sexually active people are abstinent the vast majority of the time.) Christ never commands something without giving us the resources in Him to obey.[7]

Confide in Someone

Find at least three other godly men whom you can talk to about your struggle with masturbation. Ask them to pray for you and to hold you accountable. A secret begins to lose its power when you expose it. Tell them about each day that you are able to resist. Communicate with them if you relapse. Accountability will motivate you to purity. If you know you are going to be confronted with some hard questions related to sexual purity from them, that becomes another layer of protection from acting on sinful thoughts (Ecclesiastes 4:9–12). Healing can take place in a small community of godly men. The best place for this to happen is within the relationships of a local church.

Get *Filled* with the Holy Spirit

The Holy Spirit *resides* within every believer, but we want Him to *preside* over us. The key to overcoming pornography and masturbation is to allow the Holy Spirit full access to your life. Surrender your will daily to Him, and ask Him to fill you.

Ask the Holy Spirit to show you if there are unmet spiritual, emotional, or physical needs that are driving the temptation to look at pornography and masturbate (Psalm 139:23–24). There may be a broken relationship, an unmet emotional need, undue stress, a past abandonment or abuse issue, or some other need that has not been addressed. The Holy Spirit's power is unlimited, and He will help you to overcome (see Ephesians 5:18). You can choose to submit to the Holy Spirit or submit to your sinful thought.

Give Yourself Some Grace

After all, God does. God is the God of a second chance, a God whose grace never runs out. Although God's grace is never a license for a believer to sin, grace is a reality that helps us not to despair when we relapse. God forgives you when you repent; you must also choose to forgive yourself. Stand under the faucet of God's grace, and allow Him to pour out on you a new beginning. Condemnation and shame are from the enemy. Accept God's grace (see Hebrews 4:16).

Triggers

The same triggers that cause you to view pornography are probably similar to those that lead you to masturbate. What time of the day is the temptation more intense? Where are you most likely to be tempted? Do certain people or circumstances cause you more temptation?

Think ahead of the temptation, and plan interruptions. God is faithful to provide exits prior to the enticement (1 Corinthians 10:13). Do not wait until the last moment. You must say to yourself, "I am going to do (your solution) when the temptation to view pornography and masturbate hits my mind." Every war needs a battle plan. You know you will be tempted again. You know you will be presented with another opportunity to look at pornography, to lust, to masturbate. Before that happens, decide your strategy.

Place Your Struggle on the Cross

The cross is not just a place of forgiveness, but also a place to sacrifice. God has called us to sacrifice our sinful thoughts and fantasies. As you confess your sin, nail it to the cross, and let it die. Crucifixion is painful. Giving up a sinful desire can be painful because the flesh fights hard against the will of God. Keep coming back to the cross (Colossians 2:13–14).

Pastor John Piper gives an excellent illustration in one of his messages about addressing the sin of lust in view of Jesus on the Cross:

> This is a mind war. The absolute necessity is to get the image and the impulse out of our mind.
>
> How?

Get a counter-image into the mind. Fight. Push. Strike. Don't ease up. It must be an image that is so powerful that the other image cannot survive.

There are lust-destroying images and thoughts.

For example, have you ever in the first five seconds of temptation, demanded of your mind that it look steadfastly at the crucified form of Jesus Christ? [8]

Understand This Is Unending

Your battles with lust, pornography, and masturbation will most likely continue for the rest of your life. This is not just a one-time commitment. It is important to make an initial commitment to live a pornography-free life. However, that commitment must be renewed each day, sometimes several times a day. Your daily passion for purity will be met with God's daily love for you (see Lamentations 3:21–23).

Today I challenge you to take the first step toward purity by committing to a pornography-free life. Join 1 Million Men and make your commitment.

"Sin pays—but it pays in remorse, regret and failure."

—BILLY GRAHAM—

Part 3

Keep Our Commitment

9: *Experience Freedom*

> Nobody ever did, or ever will, escape the consequences of his choices.
>
> –Alfred A. Montapert

Now that we've given you the truth about pornography in part 1 and the battle plan in part 2, we want to give you the good news here in part 3. The good news is that *any* Christian man can break free from the grips of pornography.

Notice the diagram and then the explanation:

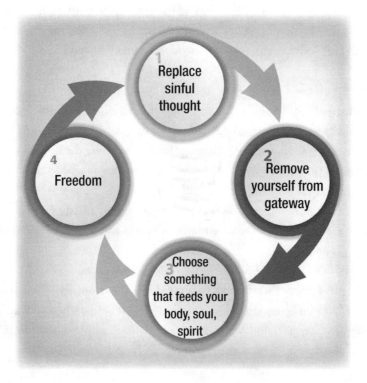

There are five steps in the process of breaking free from the bondage of pornography:

1. First, your sinful thought must be confessed immediately after it enters your mind. Tell the Lord about it, repent of it, and place it under the blood of Jesus. You cannot tolerate the sinful thought for one second. Aggressively deal with it. Surrender that thought to the authority of Jesus Christ. If you attempt to fight it on your own, most often you will lose. Jesus has all power to overcome that sinful sexual thought that is suggesting, *Look at pornography.* But as you have seen in other chapters, you cannot stop with just confessing. You must take it to the next level.

2. Second, replace your sinful thought. Quote Scripture out loud. Call an accountability person. Call a loved one or friend. Listen to Christ-centered music. Meditate on Scripture. Use the *Lectio Divina* (Sacred Reading) approach where you take the specific Scriptures you've studied and read them, reflect on God's Word, pray it back to God, and turn it into praise to Him, and then listen for the voice of the Holy Spirit to make *His* thoughts yours. Once you replace those thoughts of sin with the thoughts of God, you give God the opportunity to work in your mind and life.

3. Third, remove yourself from the gateway. A gateway is the entry point for temptation to look at pornography. If I can put it in terms of food, it would be like pulling into the parking lot of a doughnut shop, getting out of my car, standing outside, viewing the sign, smelling the doughnuts, and knowing that a few steps away I could be partaking of a hot glazed doughnut. I have placed myself in a position of easily giving in and breaking my diet. To win the victory (diet-wise), I need to immediately remove myself from that gateway. I need to get back in my car and get out of that parking lot as soon as I can!

4. Now, let's apply that to pornography. Get away from the place you are most likely to be tempted. Do something else at a time when you are most likely to view pornography. Make other plans. Remove yourself from certain people with whom you are most likely to be tempted. If you have

friends who look at pornography or are always talking dirty, stay away from them. I realize some would critically say to me, "But Jay, we need to be missionaries to those people." I'm all for evangelism, but there are ways to be a witness without subjecting yourself to people who do not value your commitment to purity.

Choose something pure that feeds your body, soul, and spirit. Incorporate spiritual disciplines, such as prayer, Bible reading, personal worship, and fasting. Exercise your body. Get enough rest. Work on developing your relationships. Read something that positively stimulates your mind. Get into community with other godly men through church. Spend time with *safe* people.

5. Finally, the fifth step is the easiest. Just experience God's freedom. When you act on God's truth, you experience God's freedom. You have God's promise on that (John 8:32)!

Pornography Free?

Yes! However, it will be one of the most difficult things you have ever done. You will have a huge battle, an intense battle, on your hands. Join1MillionMen.org is filled with resources to help you break free and stay free.

Understand this is not a one-time or one-day fix in which you never again struggle with viewing pornography. There will always be that image recorded in your mind. Satan will attempt to replay that image and tempt you to return to porn. With Satan lurking around, the road to porn is always open. You must keep it closed. You cannot go back and undo what you have seen. You don't get a redo, but you can determine from this moment forward that you will live a porn-free life. There are many men who have proven it can be done, including those featured on this series DVD.

However, you can't let down your guard for one moment. In an unguarded moment, in an unaccountable moment, you could choose to go back to porn. Our faith is based on truth and grace. The truth sets us free, and God's grace gives us the power and provision to stay free, if we continue to obey Him.

Jesus said in John 8:36, "So if the Son makes you free, you will be free indeed."

Medical scans have revealed that the brain of someone addicted to pornography mimics the brain of someone addicted to crack cocaine. Porn has been called the crack cocaine of the spirit. One of my professors, who had been sexually addicted more than 20 years earlier, allowed himself to have a brain scan while being shown pornographic images. He has been sober-minded for over 20 years and had received the permission of his accountability partners to participate in the study. The medical doctor shared with him the amazing results.

The part of the brain that reacts to pornography still lit up when he viewed the images. However, there was one noticeable difference. He did not respond with physical arousal. The brain specialist told my professor that it was as if he had an override from the brain to his body. What hope this offers! The professor said he thought about Scripture, hymns, his family, and his accountability with others while being shown these images.

Although there are times when our eyes and minds will still be assaulted by images in the world (scantily dressed women litter our billboards, TVs, and computer screens), we can win this battle with pornography through spiritual discipline, accountability, training, and continued commitment.

Do you want to be free from the bondage of pornography? Is your relationship with God important enough for you to do whatever it takes to break free from your chains? To experience God's healing power, you must answer yes to each of these questions:

1. Are you willing to be brutally honest with yourself? Breaking free requires complete transparency. No secrets, no holding back the truth about your struggle with pornography. "And you will know the truth, and the truth will make you free" (John 8:32). Exposing your secret breaks its power.

2. Are you willing to find someone with whom you can share your struggle? Someone who will honor complete confidentiality? Find a mature, God-centered man with whom you can share everything about your pornography struggle. "Therefore, confess your sins to one another, and pray for one another so that you may be healed" (James 5:16).

Bill Hybels, in *Tender Love,* makes a powerful statement about men, including Christian men:

Left to our own resources, more times than not, we will sin sexually. The pressures are just too great. That's why a vital relationship with God is critical. Without it, good sex is simply not possible. Only fully devoted, committed, authentic Christians can feel the inner tug of the Holy Spirit, the voice that tells us "Abhor evil, cling to good."

3. Do you desire God's freedom more than you desire looking at pornography? "Submit therefore to God. Resist the devil and he will flee from you. Draw near to God and He will draw near to you" (James 4:7–8). There is a high cost to experiencing freedom. It is painful, but absolutely worth it. Until you are committed to an no-matter-what-I am-going-to-break-free attitude, nothing will change. Others can help you, give you tools, and encourage you, but you alone have to be willing to do whatever it takes to break free.

4. Do you believe God will give you the strength to experience freedom over your struggle with pornography? "I can do all things through Him who strengthens me" (Philippians 4:13). "Now to Him who is able to do far more abundantly beyond all that we ask or think, according to the power that works within us" (Ephesians 3:20). As you come to our omnipotent God and place your faith in Him, He will give you the strength to overcome. Believe it.

5. Are you willing to come clean with your spouse and fully disclose your pornography struggle? "But speaking the truth in love, we are to grow up in all aspects into Him" (Ephesians 4:15). For you to experience freedom, you absolutely must be transparent with your wife. Keeping this secret will hurt her far worse than sharing it with her. God works in an atmosphere of transparency.

6. Are you willing to embrace God's truth, realizing that it is the only way to experience freedom from pornography? "If we say that we have no sin, we are deceiving ourselves and the truth is not in us. If we confess our sins, He is faithful and righteous to forgive us our sins and to cleanse us from all unrighteousness" (1 John 1:8–9).

7. Do you believe you will experience God's freedom if you act on what God says? "The Lord knows how to rescue the godly from temptation" (2 Peter 2:9). If God is omnipresent, omnipotent, and omniscient, then He has the power to do exactly what He says He will do.

If you said yes and meant it, I assure you, by the authority of God's Word, that you can experience freedom. I equally assure you that it will not be easy, nor can you simply sign a card and get on with your life. Freedom is a daily battle. There is never an occasion where you can let down your shield.

10: Commit with Others

You may have to fight a battle more than once to win it.

—Margaret Thatcher

Sin is not hurtful because it is forbidden, but it is forbidden because it is hurtful.

—Benjamin Franklin

This commitment to live pornography free will change our lives and our future. We have learned about the destructive consequences that viewing pornography has on our relationships with God, wife, and family. Further, pornography's skewed view of women shows us not only why this enemy is dangerous, but also what could happen if we do not choose to live without pornography.

Making the porn-free commitment is your way of drawing a line in the sand and saying, "On this day I begin a journey of living pornography free." That process begins by telling God of your intentions and asking Him for daily strength and resolve. You will want to read the commitment, sign it, and then place your name on the virtual wall at Join1MillionMen.org. You will be joining along with other Christian men from churches across the nation and world, who are willing to draw that line in the sand and declare, "I will live pornography free!"

Porn-Free Commitment

Here's the basic commitment you will find online:

- ❏ I am making a lifetime commitment to being porn free, knowing this commitment is kept one day at a time.

- ❏ I am acknowledging that I have the capacity to be tempted by pornography and could give in to that temptation at any time.

- ❏ I am placing my relationship with God as the number one priority of my life, and I admit that God cannot be number one if I am viewing pornography.

- ❏ I am placing my relationship with my wife (if married) as my number two priority. I admit that she cannot be that priority in my life, and that I cannot love her like I should, if I am viewing pornography.

- ❏ I am placing my relationship with my children (if you have children) as the number three priority in my life. I admit they cannot be that priority in my life, and that I cannot love them like I should, if I am viewing pornography.

- ❏ I understand the only power I have over pornography is given by the Holy Spirit as I am surrendered to Him.

- ❏ I will have at least three other men I can call at any hour of the day or night when the thought enters my mind to look at pornography.

- ❏ I will consider the consequences to my walk with God, my relationship with my wife (if married) and children (if any), my other family members, my job, and everything that is important to me when the thought enters my mind to look at pornography.

- ❏ I will do everything possible to create a porn-free environment. (Possible examples are: screensaver of my wife (if married) and children (if any); pictures of wife and children around the computer; use of the computer in an open place where anyone can see; download accountability software on my computer; install filtering software on my computer; share my computer password with my wife or friend; put Scriptures on screensaver; put sticky notes with Scriptures on computer; take a different route to work to avoid temptation; when staying in a hotel, ask the front desk to turn off pay-per-view on the cable; if necessary, avoid traveling with my laptop and instead use computer in hotel business center; and eliminate the premium cable channels on my television).

❏ I will develop the spiritual disciplines of Bible reading daily, prayer, personal worship, small-group Bible study, church attendance, fasting, meditating, and journaling (recording what God is saying to you through His Word or the Holy Spirit, and free writing about your personal victories and failures).

❏ I will recognize those times and places when I am most likely to look at pornography and interrupt them by taking specific steps to guard my mind and heart.

❏ I will immediately remove pornography from my life by destroying any porn of any kind.

❏ Because I am not alone in my struggle, I will pray for and seek to help my brothers in Christ to stay pure.

❏ I will seek help, if needed, from a Christian counselor and support group.

❏ I will review and renew this commitment daily.

Signed _____

Date _____

Prayer

Prayer connects you with the One who has all power, is everywhere present (all at once and all the time), and knows everything past, present, and future. He knows where, when, and how you are most tempted. As you call on Him, He gives you a sense of power and peace, and a spirit of overcoming that temptation. Use prayer to help yourself and to help others who are struggling with pornography.

> He who has learned to pray has learned the greatest secret of a happy and holy life.
>
> —William Law

> Jesus is strong . . . but He's also approachable. He is able to carry our load . . . but He'll never make us feel embarrassed or defeated for asking.
>
> —Joni Eareckson Tada

11: *R*ecruit *Our Sons*

What If I Find My Son Has Been Viewing Pornography?

We look at this issue more closely in the book for wives and on our movement Web site. But we could not complete this book for men without calling attention to our boys, our sons.

Pornography is a potential and probable problem for every home—even your Christian home. If you have a computer, cell phone, television, DVD player, or radio in your home, pornography has a gateway, a portal. In other words, you must be very proactive in guarding these portals. Whether you have a 10-year-old or an older teenager, there is some information you as a parent need to embrace, as painful as that might be.

To hope that your child will never be exposed to pornography is truly wishful thinking. Yes, you do everything you can to protect your child by setting up safeguards (such as Internet filtering and accountability software), and helping your child choose friends wisely. However, there is almost a 100 percent chance that your child will be exposed to some type of pornography. It is not a matter of *if*, but *when*.

Children are being introduced to computers prior to entering preschool between the ages of two and four. Prepare yourself now for the inevitabilities of what your son will be exposed to through media and society. Equip yourself with ways you can respond to him with truth and grace, not guilt and shame, in order to protect him. The younger-aged child especially will feel shame by the time you discover he has been exposed to pornography.

Fathers are responsible for the spiritual growth and protection of their children, for bringing them up in the training and instruction of the Lord (Ephesians 6:4). For men with sons, that includes informing them and protecting them from sexual brokenness, which often begins with viewing pornography.

While not discounting the possibility that a daughter might view pornography, by far this is a male-dominant issue presently (although girls are increasingly viewing porn).

Every Christian father needs to understand the power and pull of the temptation for his son to view pornography. We simply cannot afford to let our feelings of embarrassment or awkwardness prevent us from sharing with our sons the truth about their number one temptation. Dads need to create an atmosphere where their sons feel safe to talk to them about sexual matters. That is the father's responsibility—not the son's—to take the initiative.

Statistical research supports the need for fathers to address pornography early on:

• The average age of first exposure is 11 years old.
• 80 percent of boys 15 to 17 years old have multiple hard-core exposures.
• 90 percent of boys 8 to 16 years old have viewed porn online.
• Over 30 percent of boys 16 to 17 years old intentionally visited X-rated sites in the past year.[1]
• The largest group of pornography consumers is 12- to 17-year-old boys.[2]
• 12-year-old boys are at the most detrimental age for exposure to pornography and/or sexual abuse.[3]

In most cases, the child unintentionally accessed the sex sites, often in the process of doing homework and using a seemingly innocent-sounding word to search for information or pictures.

As a parent, you must do everything possible to prevent your child from seeing pornography. You have to know that there is a built-in curiosity about sexual things in a young man's mind. When you combine that with the fact that pornography is pervasive on the Internet and that our culture is becoming *pornified* (pornography is part of the mainstream culture), your son will no doubt be exposed to it. So what is a father to do?

Watch God's Word Together

Give your son a scriptural basis for living a life of sexual purity. The following verses, all from the New Living Translation, are helpful:

You say, "Food was made for the stomach, and the stomach for food." (This is true, though someday God will do away with both of them.) But you can't say that our bodies were made for sexual immorality. They were made for the Lord, and the Lord cares about our bodies (1 Corinthians 6:13).

Run from sexual sin! No other sin as clearly affects the body as this one does. For sexual immorality is a sin against your own body. Don't you realize that your body is the temple of the Holy Spirit, who lives in you and was given to you by God? You do not belong to yourself, for God bought you with a high price. So you must honor God with your body (18–20).

And so, dear brothers and sisters, I plead with you to give your bodies to God because of all he has done for you. Let them be a living and holy sacrifice—the kind he will find acceptable. This is truly the way to worship him. Don't copy the behavior and customs of this world, but let God transform you into a new person by changing the way you think. Then you will learn to know God's will for you, which is good and pleasing and perfect (Romans 12:1–2).

Give honor to marriage, and remain faithful to one another in marriage. God will surely judge people who are immoral and those who commit adultery (Hebrews 13:4).

God's will is for you to be holy, so stay away from all sexual sin. Then each of you will control his own body and live in holiness and honor—not in lustful passion like the pagans who do not know God and his ways (1 Thessalonians 4:3–5).

I made a covenant with my eyes not to look with lust at a young woman (Job 31:1).

Turn my eyes from worthless things, and give me life through your word (Psalm 119:37).

A Porn–Free Home

Freedom includes guarding what enters your home through the Internet, premium cable television, other questionable television programs, magazines, books, or movies. Never tolerate any kind of pornography. If there is any porn in your home, destroy it immediately. Outside of the fact that no Christian should possess pornography, your child is guaranteed to find it.

Install Software

You need both Internet filtering and accountability programs on your computer. One screens and the other informs an accountability partner (or parent) of Internet activity. There are several good programs for both. Covenant Eyes has very effective programs. Go to covenanteyes.com and check out the options. You love your child too much to trust him or her with a world that promotes "Have sex now!" Your investment in this software is worth far more than the nominal price you will pay.

Talk with Your Son

Let him know about the dangers of pornography, and tell him why you are installing the software. You are not distrusting your son; however, you are distrusting those on the Internet whose purpose is to hook every young man. The porn industry focuses on the young, attempting to develop consumers for life.

Ask Your Son

Find out whether your son has been exposed to pornography. Assure him you won't be angry if he says yes. You need to find out how he was exposed. Was it on the home computer? Was it at a friend's house? Ask him how it made him feel. Ask him if his friends are looking at pornography.

Have the Talk

If you have not had "the talk" with him about sex, it's now time. My strong encouragement is to talk with your son before he reaches the age of ten, if not sooner. You know your child and his level of maturity. You do not want your son learning the facts of life from Internet pornography. There are good resources available, such as:

Resources for Talking to Your Child About Sex

- *A Chicken's Guide to Talking Turkey with Your Kids About Sex,* by Kevin Leman
- *How and When to Tell Your Kids About Sex: A Lifelong Approach to Shaping Your Child's Sexual Character (God's Design for Sex),* by Brenna Jones and Stan Jones
- *Teaching Your Children Healthy Sexuality: A Biblical Approach to Preparing Them for Life,* by Jim Burns
- *Before I Was Born (God's Design for Sex),* by Carolyn Nystrom
- *How God Makes Babies,* by Jim Burns (For Ages 6 to 9)
- *What's the Big Deal? Why God Cares About Sex (God's Design for Sex),* by Brenna Jones
- *Talking to Your Kids About Sex: How to Have a Lifetime of Age-Appropriate Conversations with Your Children About Healthy Sexuality,* by Dr. Mark Laaser
- *Every Teenager's Little Black Book on Sex and Dating,* by Blaine Bartel

Explain the Dangers

Tell him how harmful pornography is and how looking at it is very displeasing to God. As a follower of Jesus, you should teach him that God gave sex as a gift only to those who are married. What your son saw in that pornographic image goes against everything God wants. Let him know that intentionally looking at porn is a sin against God, that it harms women, and negatively impacts every person who looks at it. Help your son to understand the four reasons pornography is so dangerous—accessible, anonymous (at least it promises to be secretive), affordable (much of it is free), and addictive.

Set Internet Boundaries

You should establish specific times for your children to use the Internet. You need to control those times. Make sure the computer is located in an open area. Reinforce to them that you will see the history of where they have gone. If by accident they run across a pornographic image, they should immediately let you know. Also, teach them to *never, ever* give out personal information on the Internet (name, address, phone number, or email address). Remind them there are people who would and could hurt them with this information. Parents, you cannot be too careful here!

Also, monitor Facebook, MySpace, and other social networks where your child could be exposed. Monitor cell phone usage as well. Warn him against sexting (texting sexual materials).

Guard Passwords

You must never allow your child to change the password into the Internet account unless you know about it. Parent, you are the controller of the computer.

Identify the Boundaries

Clearly communicate the boundaries concerning the Internet. Let your child know that, if those boundaries are crossed, there will be discipline. Spell out the discipline prior to an offense.

Find the Source

If you discover pornography viewed by your son, ask him how he found it. Give him the opportunity to tell you exactly what happened. Don't shame your child. Instead, share with him that the image he saw is not what God wants.

Accidents Will Happen

If he accidently sees a pornographic image, your son is to come and tell you immediately. Assure him he won't get in trouble. But let him know the consequences if he sees an image and doesn't report it. Encourage him to talk to God about it and to ask God to help him to never see that kind of image again.

You Can't Always Be There

Talk with your son about how to respond if he is at a friend's house and sees pornography. Coach him to walk out of the room and call you. It is vital that you help your son choose friends whose parents share your core values. If you discover that the friend's father willingly exposes his son to porn, you must deal seriously with this. Clearly communicate to your son that this may mean never again going into that home, never again associating with that family. Keep in mind that 67 percent of men now say porn is acceptable.

0

Spiritual Disciplines

Lead your son to practice worship, Bible study and meditation, prayer, fasting, church attendance, and serving someone through ministry. Practicing these disciplines builds strong walls of protection around any child of God. Of course, fathers must set the example.

Joint Commit

Challenge your son, at the appropriate age, to make the Pornography-Free Commitment. In fact, make that commitment together.

Patrick F. Fagan, PhD, in his study, *The Effects of Pornography on Individuals, Marriage, Family and Community,* says,

> The main defenses against pornography are close family life, a good marriage and good relations between parents and children, coupled with deliberate parental monitoring of Internet use.[4]

Dad, God has called you to take the lead.

12: *R*emain Free

Our main purpose in this project is to bring the issue of pornography and its consequences onto the stage of every church. Then, we want to provide a way for men to overcome. Secrecy about this problem is destroying Christian men, Christian families, and churches all over the world. And it will only get worse until we bring our pornographic practices out into the light and defeat them.

Satan has convinced many pastors and Christian leaders that the subject of pornography is just too sensitive and too offensive to speak about from the pulpit. But there is porn in the pew. It's there, but men are so ashamed, and they think they are alone in their struggle.

The Greek word for pornography, which basically means "writings about prostitutes," identifies that this was a practice of using writings as a means to arouse a person sexually. Used in a broader sense today, pornography includes any sexual image or activity that arouses a person sexually. Pornography is easily delivered through the Internet, cell phones, premium cable channels, On Demand or pay-per-view movies, magazines, DVDs, and any other means the porn industry can and will think of to deliver in the future, as we have shown in earlier chapters.

According to Family Safe Media, pornography recently became a $97 billion industry worldwide, including the $13 billion dollar industry that's in the United States alone. According to statistics, pornography revenue exceeds the combined revenues of all professional baseball, football, and basketball franchises, and the combined revenues of ABC, CBS, and NBC.[1] It even has larger revenues than Microsoft, Google, Amazon, eBay, Yahoo, Apple, and Netflix combined!

Craig Gross, Founder of XXXChurch.com, says in his book *Eyes of Integrity*, "Lurking behind every screen in your home is a portal of devastating potential." "No one is outside the reach of porn's grip."

Dr. Richard Land, as president of the Ethics and Religious Liberty Commission of the Southern Baptist Convention, said:

> Christians and the Gospel ministry have not escaped the reach of porn. Internet pornography is in your church. If your church has got more than 50 members, it's in your church. I can tell you hardcore pornography is on the seminary campus. It's on the Christian college campus. It's in the pastorate. It's on the staff.[2]

If you are struggling, there are some things I know about you. You feel shame and guilt. You have probably tried to quit the habit hundreds of times. You feel you are the only Christian man struggling with this. You are fearful your wife will find out. You feel your moral authority has been emasculated. You feel trapped. You feel a mighty pull, an attraction that is both detestable and exciting, abhorrent and attractive.

Although the Bible does not specifically deal with every issue, it does deal with them through principles—timeless truths transcending cultures. Let me illustrate. Nowhere in the Bible does it say, "Thou shalt not log onto that XXX site!" "Thou shalt not visit Adult Friend Finder." But the Bible does address the issue of pornography clearly, as we have reviewed carefully.

I have attempted to speak here to men who love God, men who want to do the right thing, men who have a testimony of salvation, men who do love their wives and families, men who feel great shame and guilt for viewing pornography. These are the men I want to address and help.

For those men who say "It couldn't happen to me," I quote Bill Perkins, who hosts fantastic writing and conference ministries for men:

> If you think you cannot fall into sexual sin, then you're godlier than David, stronger than Samson, and wiser than Solomon.

Whether it's your son, dad, your, friend, co-worker, fellow brother in Christ, or you, each of us men knows someone who is struggling with porn. Guaranteed! If you are struggling with viewing porn, Satan wants you to believe that you are the only One. I assure you that you are not. Satan wants you chained to shame and guilt. Jesus wants to set you free through His amazing grace. Jesus died and rose from the dead so you could live free!

Join 1 Million Men is a movement for the average Christian man who is struggling at some level with lust and pornography, to join with others in the battle. This movement opens the way for a plan for success, including for a new generation who need to hear *God's* perspective of sexuality—instead of learning sex from the enemy territory of a porn site, and becoming a prisoner to sexual addiction.

This movement is also for those men who don't struggle. Your commitment sets the example for sons and daughters and for other brothers in Christ. It is a confession that says, "Yes I could go there, but I pledge that by the grace and power of a resurrected Savior, I won't go there, and I will reach out to others who need help."

However, for the man who *has* become addicted to pornography, failure is certain until that man addresses what is driving his addiction. This movement is a hand reaching out to every Christian man, so each man can grab hold and begin to address his level of struggle.

Scripture is completely effective and powerful to help men experience breakthrough freedom from any bondage. Yet, there is also a need for understanding how the human mind and emotions work. Those who require more extensive methods of help can begin to get that help.

I have had the privilege of sitting through Dr. Mark Laaser's intensive workshop for men. I have seen the pain and the commitment involved in a willingness to go to those places where addiction has found a root—an unmet need. There is a definite connection between the addiction and a man's life traumas and resulting emotional wounds.

Traumas become seedbeds for addictions unless they are addressed in a healthy, biblical way. That requires a lot of hard work, time, accountability, and a desire that exceeds one's default feeling. While it would be impossible to expect that a man could change all that on his own, Join 1 Million Men is a beginning commitment—a first step—not the final end-all; a step among many forward steps in experiencing freedom. Remaining free is a daily choice.

When there are addiction issues, God provides for additional steps in the process of healing. If we can reach the Christian man before he is addicted, we have a greater opportunity for freedom. Again, an addiction is often the consequence of a past wound or trauma not being addressed in a healthy, God-directed way. The addictive behavior results initially and perhaps primarily, from wrong belief systems. Those beliefs can be true, perceived truths, or lies; but they have power over what we do. Initially, truth about feelings needs to be understood, and perceived truth and lies need to be revealed. Freedom begins with understanding the truth.

Join 1 Million Men is a step toward revealing Satan's lies and helping Christian men understand how God's truth can set them free. Yet, when it comes to addiction, multiple weapons need to be accessed in order to remain free. Dr. Laaser says these weapons or, in his terminology, "tools," won't heal your addiction, but will get you to a place where God can work in your life. He lists: positive self-care; gaining information about addiction and trauma; accountability to others, to self, to wife, and to God; twelve-steps; journaling; counseling; and medication (if necessary).

Understanding the difference between guilt and shame is another essential piece to understanding freedom. Guilt is a feeling resulting from *doing* something wrong; whereas shame is a feeling of *being* something wrong—what I have *done* versus who I *am*. Satan keeps many Christian men in bondage because they believe their struggle or addiction cannot be helped. They think it is who they *are*. Removing that false belief is a key for that man to break free. My prayer is that Join 1 Million Men will be the open hand you grab ahold of, and although it's not the cure, you can begin to mount up to make commitment to a process of freedom. "Therefore, to one who knows the right thing to do and does not do it, to him it is sin" (James 4:17).

For pastors and Christian leaders within the local church, Join 1 Million Men presents us the right thing to do. It gives a pastor the tool to start the discussion with less awkwardness.

Christian men should be involved in accountability relationships within the local church. Finding a group that specifically deals with sexual integrity issues is a significant step toward experiencing real freedom in this area. For those who are struggling, a support group is essential to experience healing. Don't remain in isolation.

You will want to attempt to find this support group system in your church. If unavailable, find a local, Bible-teaching church in your community or region that does have one. It is that important. Check out the church's Web site to determine what it offers by way of support groups.

The church is exactly the place where we should be talking about sex. When the timeless truth of Scriptural principles is presented in the power of the Holy Spirit, God has an opportunity to work. We can get the conversation started in churches, support groups, accountability groups, conferences, workshops, and through counseling.

In face-to-face conversations with multiple national Christian ministries, I have spoken to each one about the frustration of trying to gain entrance within the local church. Join 1 Million Men is an instrument to open that door so other specific ministries can effectively work. The fact is, if we don't get in the door of the local church, we won't win! Please join us in this battle that we are winning, in Jesus' name. No one gets better by trying to do this without help. Visit Join1MillionMen.org now! And spend some time getting familiar with the resources listed below. They can offer you invaluable help as you strive to remain free.

Accountability and Monitoring Software

Covenant Eyes — covenanteyes.com

X3watch PRO — x3watch.com

Computer Cop — computercop.com

Family Cyber Alert — itcompany.com/cyberalert.htm

Guardian Monitor — guardiansoftware.com

McGruff Safeguard — gomcgruff.com

Filtering and Parental Control Software

Safe Families Web blocker — safefamilies.org

ContentProtect — contentwatch.com

Safe Eyes — Internetsafety.com

CyberPatrol — cyberpatrol.com

Cybersitter — cybersitter.com

Norton Internet Security — us.norton.com/Internet-security

Net Nanny — netnanny.com

McAfee Internet Security — home.mcafee.com

Christian Support Groups

Celebrate Recovery — celebraterecovery.com
L.I.F.E. Ministries International — freedomeveryday.org

Books

Healing the Wounds of Sexual Addiction, Dr. Mark Laaser
Shattered Vows, Debra Laaser
Porn Free Church, Covenant Eyes.com
The Porn Trap, Wendy and Larry Maltz
Don't Call It Love, Patrick Carnes
In the Shadows of the Net, Patrick Carnes, David Delmonico, Elizabeth Griffin
When Good Men Are Tempted, Bill Perkins
Eyes of Integrity: The Porn Pandemic and How It Affects You, Craig Gross
The Drug of the New Millennium: The Brain Science Behind Internet Pornography Use, Mark B. Kastleman

Web sites:

PornHarms.org
Faithfulandtrueministries.com
XXXChurch.com
ThePinkCross.org
Healthysex.com
Bethesdaworkshops.org
Freedomeveryday.org (L.I.F.E. Ministries International)
SA.org (Sexaholics Anonymous)

Your Gift of Salvation

John said, "But to all who believed him and accepted him, he gave the right to become children of God" (John 1:12 NLT).

This Scripture indicates there is a specific time and place where Jesus Christ comes into your life, and when He does He gives you overcoming, bondage-breaking power.

Salvation takes place the moment you place your faith and trust in Jesus Christ alone as your Savior and turn away from your sin and receive Him. You have resurrection power in your life. Once you experience salvation, you have the capacity to say Yes to God's will and No to the temptation to sin, because you have His Spirit.

Now, I want to ask you the most important question you will ever be asked: Do you know that you know if you died right now you would go to heaven? Today, you can make absolutely sure by opening your heart and inviting Jesus Christ in. I invite you to pray this prayer and mean it in your heart right now and begin the journey of a lifetime:

Dear God,

I confess to You that I have sinned; I have broken Your commandments. I know that I cannot save myself. I can't be good enough nor work my way to heaven. Jesus, that's why You came and lived a perfect life. You went to the Cross for me and took my sin on Yourself. You shed Your blood, You died, and You rose from the dead. I trust You alone for my salvation what You did on the Cross—not what I can do. I turn from my sin and ask You to forgive me. I turn to You and receive You into my life as my Savior and Lord. Write my name in Your Book . . . the Lamb's Book of Life.

In Jesus' name. Amen."

I encourage you to access God's amazing power through prayer, reading God's Word, getting involved in a Bible-centered church, private and corporate worship, and obedience to God's commands. As you practice your faith, you will daily be strengthened to live a godly life.

*U*sing this in your small group with Our Hardcore Battle Plan *DVD*

Imagine with me millions of men in churches of all sizes, and in multiple denominations—men who commit to a pornography-free lifestyle! I believe we would see revival as we have not experienced in our lifetime.

We are waging a war—and our mission is to free Christian men from pornography. Ours is a grace-based response to men engaged in this prevalent struggle, rather than a shame-based condemnation of those who are ensnared. To share this information, plan, and commitment opportunity that has already helped thousands, so that at least 1 million Christian men say, "I will take Jesus seriously about what He said, "The pure in heart will see God," (Matthew 5:8).

For men to see God work in their lives, their marriages, and families, their hearts must be pure. Our heart cannot be pure if pornography is part of our life. Pornography destroys our intimacy with God. Christian men must commit to reject porn for Christ's sake and our own good.

Many of us would like nothing more than to shut down the pornography industry and to see organized boycotts against this evil, although every Christian man should boycott anything the pornography industry promotes. Sadly, there is so much interconnection through the Internet, television, movies, and other types of porn providers that it is literally impossible to boycott it all. But we are not making excuses.

Christian men have the edge; the Holy Spirit resides within us. When a man allows the Holy Spirit to *preside*, freedom is attained and can be maintained, and pornography defeated. Truth sets free and grace confirms and maintains that freedom.

Having dealt with men as well as their wives and families who are wounded by pornography, all searching for healing, I made some critical discoveries. I was looking for materials to help our men at First Baptist Church at the Mall, Lakeland, Florida, (FBC) the church I have been privileged to lead since

February of 1996. There are good materials, written by parachurch organizations, counselors, and academics. However, I was seeking material truly written from the heart of a senior pastor. That's when God convicted me to learn all I could and to write this material. Truth-based and grace-driven; bold yet sensitive and understanding of this very challenging subject inside the church.

I prepared materials to meet the needs of the men in my church and initially asked men to gather with me for six Wednesday evening sessions. I made the commitment to full disclosure, to hold back nothing as it related to sexual issues and pornography. The response, honestly, surprised me.

On the third week, during the conclusion of the teaching time, I asked our men to stand if they were struggling with pornography. The far majority of the men (about 300) stood to their feet. Though all of us had our eyes closed and head bowed, I could hear the sound of many theater seats hitting the backs of the chairs. I thought, this sounds like the beginning of freedom.

The best way to describe it: there was a spirit of revival that broke out among our men, and this was the beginning of a journey that continues to affect the men, marriages, and families of our church—and our service to others so positively. Men who have achieved some victory in Christ are helping other men.

Very important, I added an additional evening to speak only to the women, to whom the women's book in this series is directed. In addition I asked our parents to come together as I shared a teaching on "Protecting Your Child from Sexual Brokenness," Which is a crucial component to help the next generation win in this continuing war.

My observation is that the church is waiting for its leaders to address these issues. There will always be some who will be critical of leaders who speak of sexual issues in the church, but future generations depend upon the Christians today to stand individually and say, "I will live a pornography free life."

I asked our men to make a commitment to live a pornography-free life. I felt it was important to encourage not only the men who were struggling with pornography to make the commitment, but also those who do not struggle. I told them to "draw a line in the sand to share with your family and friends that you are making a commitment to never go there!"

This is something every church of any size and denomination can do. The commitment card had a perforated portion where the part with a man's name was prominent and then the bottom portion was kept for our records. We built a huge wall in the lobby of our church to display all the commitment cards signed by our men. We wanted wives, families, and other men in the church to see the obvious commitment. At this writing, more than 1,300 men's names are on the wall.

The wall has become an opportunity for our church to discuss this sensitive issue. The door has been opened to demonstrate publicly our men's passion for purity. And this challenge has become a movement that is now reaching churches beyond FBC Lakeland.

We want you! We challenge you, as a follower of Jesus Christ, to "join us on the wall," to make a commitment that from this day forward you will live porn free.

We encourage you to access our *Hardcore Battle Plan* DVD, which will provide you with additional content that guides you in using each component of this movement and series in your church or other small group.

Drawing your line in the sand begins when you tell God of your intentions and ask Him for daily strength and resolve. Read the commitment, make the commitment, and then remain accountable to God, yourself, and to others.

*E*ndnotes

Chapter 1

[1]"Pornography and the Average Joe," Baylor University Counseling Center, n.d., http://www.baylor.edu/counseling_center/baretruth/index.php?id=35783 (accessed April 17, 2013).

[2]David Roach, "Pastors: Porn a Big Problem Among Members," Baptist Press, November 10, 2011, http://www.bpnews.net/bpnews.asp?id=36528 (accessed April 15, 2013).

Chapter 2

[1]City-Data.com, "Has Porn Destroyed Our Society?," City-Data Forum, http://www.city-data.com/forum/non-romantic-relationships/1794427-has-porn-destroyed-our-society-we.html (accessed April 18, 2013).

Chapter 3

[1]Mary Eberstadt and Mary Anne Layden, *The Social Costs of Pornography* (Princeton, NJ: The Witherspoon Institute, 2010), 23.

Chapter 4

[1]Steven Stack, Ira Wasserman, and Roger Kern, "Adult Social Bonds and Use of Internet Pornography," *Social Science Quarterly* 85 (2004): 75–88.

JOIN
MEN

²Beatriz Lia Avila Mileham, "Online Infidelity in Internet Chat Rooms: An Ethnographic Exploration" (diss., University of Florida, 2003), http://www .marriagemissions.com/quotes-on-pornography-and-cybersex/ (accessed April 16, 2013).

³Stuart Vogelman, "Does Porn or a Husband's Wandering Eyes Hurt a Marriage?," http://www.marriagemissions.com/quotes-on-pornography-and-cybersex/ (accessed April 16, 2013).

Chapter 8

¹Cory Silverberg, "Myths About Masturbation," sexuality.about.com/od/masturbation/tp/masturbationmyt.htm, updated January 19, 2009 (accessed April 19, 2013).

²Archibald D. Hart, *The Sexual Man* (Nashville: W Publishing Group, 1994), 119, http://www.provenmen.org/framework/index.php?page=need (accessed April 23, 2013).

³Ibid., 95.

⁴"Effects of Porn Addiction," All About Life Challenges, http://www .allaboutlifechallenges.org/effects-of-porn-addiction-faq.htm (accessed April 19, 2013).

⁵Hart, *The Sexual Man*, 140.

⁶Lou Priolo, *The Complete Husband* (Amityville, NY: Calvary Press, 1999), 173.

⁷Randy Alcorn, "How Can I Overcome Masturbation?," http://www.epm.org/resources/2010/Mar/18/how-can-i-overcome-masturbation/ (accessed April 19, 2013).

[8]John Piper, "A Passion for Purity Versus Passsive Prayers," November 10, 1999, www.desiringgod.org (accessed April 22, 2013). ©2013 Desiring God Foundation. Used by permission.

Chapter 11

[1]The Ethics and Religious Liberty Commission, "Pornography: Quick Facts: Reliable and Informative Snapshots of the Focus Issue," http://erlc.com/issues/quick-facts/por (accessed April 22, 2013).

[2]Eric Dye, "The Staggering Stats of Pornography," Churchm.ag, http://churchm.ag/porn-stats (accessed April 22, 2013).

[3]Craig Georgianna, Tom Underhill, Chad Kelland, *Hyperstimulation* (Brea, CA: The Center for Psychotherapy, 2010), 169–70.

[4]Patrick F. Fagan, PhD, "The Effects of Pornography on Individuals, Marriage, Family and Community," Family Research Council, December 2009, http://www.frc.org/pornography-effects (accessed April 22, 2013).

Chapter 12

[1]http://www.familysafemedia.com/pornography_statistics.html (accessed April 24, 2013).

[2]Tom Strode, "Porn's Destruction Is Infiltrating the Church," Baptist Press, May 27, 2011, http://www.bpnews.net/bpnews.asp?id=35406 (accessed April 24, 2013).

New Hope® Publishers is a division of WMU®, an international organization that challenges Christian believers to understand and be radically involved in God's mission. For more information about WMU, go to wmu.com. More information about New Hope books may be found at NewHopeDigital.com. New Hope books may be purchased at your local bookstore.

Use the QR reader on your
smartphone to visit us online at
NewHopeDigital.com

If you've been blessed by this book, we would like to hear your story. The publisher and author welcome your comments and suggestions at: newhopereader@wmu.org.

SET 1 FREE

WORLDCRAFTS

WorldCrafts^{SM} develops sustainable, fair-trade businesses among impoverished people around the world.

The WorldCrafts Set1Free campaign actively empowers WorldCrafts buyers and aids artisans by highlighting those groups involved in human trafficking and sexual exploitation.

Learn more about the campaign, purchase products in the campaign, download our prayer guide, and learn how to mobilize others by going to WorldCrafts.org/Set1Free.asp.

WORLDCRAFTS℠

Committed. Holistic. Fair Trade.

WorldCrafts.org 1-800-968-7301

WorldCrafts is a division of WMU®